HAWICK
AMATEUR
OPERATIC
SOCIETY

Affiliated to the National Operatic
& Dramatic Association

On With The Show

One Hundred Years Of Hawick Amateur Operatic Society

A Pictorial History

Ian W. Seeley

Cover design by Derek Lunn

Cover photograph - Dancers in *Oklahoma* – 1955. (l-r) Kitty Douglas, Cathie Hay, Nancy Aitken and Evelyn Kersel

Published by Hawick Amateur Operatic Society 2010

Text Copyright © Ian W. Seeley 2010

ISBN 978-0-9567375-0-2

Printed and bound for HAOS by
Scott & Paterson Ltd.
9 High Street, Hawick
2010

FOREWORD

It is a great honour and privilege to be asked to write the foreword to this wonderful book; a 'Pictorial History' of our local Amateur Operatic Society.

As Hawick AOS President for 2010-2011 and NODA (National Operatic and Dramatic Association) Borders Representative in Scotland, I am very excited to be involved in all the Centenary Celebrations.

My own membership of the Society has spanned a mere forty of these hundred years, but many fond memories of the Society, family and friends make the history within these pages something to treasure.

To reach a one hundredth birthday alone is an exceptional achievement, but to be able to produce such an inspired, in-depth, historical account of the Society seemed to be an almost insurmountable challenge given the scattered nature of the documentation. It therefore, unquestionably, gives me immense pleasure to be able to thank the person who has made this publication possible.

Mr. Seeley, as he was always known to me and to hundreds of his pupils at Hawick High School, is, I am thrilled to say, a mentor to myself and to many people throughout the Hawick Community. In order to put words on the page and names to each picture, he has spent hundreds of hours researching and interviewing past members of our society. Hundreds of names and local associations have been recognised to make the reading of this book absolutely fascinating. No stone has been left unturned.

The book could not have been produced in this form without Ian Seeley's painstaking approach to his task, and I offer him, on behalf of the Society, many thanks and congratulations.

I know, also, that in this project, Ian has had the unstinting support of his wife, Alison, herself an ardent Society member, and that he would be the first to concede that the book has benefited from her advice and constructive criticism.

Whatever sleepless nights Ian may have endured worrying about whose name or contribution he may have been omitted, I am sure that these will be outweighed by the pleasure generated from the smiles, laughter and, in some cases, tears, evoked by this truly honest and informative account of our Society's first one hundred years.

It only remains for me to repeat a massive, resounding THANK YOU! And so, 'On With The Show!'

Deborah Lyons, President

PREFACE

In compiling this pictorial history of Hawick Amateur Operatic Society (HAOS), emphasis has been placed upon the identity of the Society and its members within the local community. To this end it has been an important principle to try, as far as possible, to put names to the images. The view has been taken that an unnamed photograph of a company or persons, for example, is of diminished value for the simple reason that, objectively, it could come from any operatic society in Britain.

The present volume seeks to honour those who have contributed to the Society`s continued existence and success over one hundred years. Over twelve hundred people have performed with the Society. Obviously, they cannot all be mentioned in the main text and photographs but their contribution is recorded in the `first appearance` listings at the back of the book. It has also been deemed important to link identities, where possible, to the community through family, occupational and social ties in order that the reader may make the necessary connections. Otherwise, unless the pictures are specific to one`s own connection with HAOS, they are meaningless.

There is a poignancy in the preservation of these images because they are reminders of our own human transience. The vibrant young men and women of the `teens, `twenties and `thirties whose striking looks and postures engage our interest have passed away, but many townsfolk will recall some of them as Hawick personalities in their heyday – people who brought colour and distinctiveness to the `grey auld toon` in varied spheres of interest, be they the workplace, in sport and recreation or in the Common-Riding.

The HAOS story is a paradigm of our own lives – a series of entrances and exits mingled with joy, sadness and pathos – and it is hoped that these images and the accompanying text may evoke pleasant memories of people who derived enormous pleasure from their hobby and who also gave it in good measure.

IWS

AUTHOR`S ACKNOWLEDGMENTS

It would have been impossible to create this volume without the generosity and trust of those who so willingly lent me relevant material in the form of photographs, past programmes and newspaper and magazine cuttings. The positive encouragement of many former and present members of the Society has been invaluable. Accordingly, I wish to express my thanks to Mrs. Evelyn Aitken, Mrs. Eileen Aitkin, Mrs. Mina Carruthers, Mrs. Letta Dalgleish, Mrs. Shelagh Duncan, Mrs. Nan Gibb, Mrs. Sheila Henderson, Miss. Betty Howarth, Mrs. Dorothy Inglis, Mrs. Margaret Logan, Ms. Deborah Lyons, the late Mrs. Ella McLeod, Mrs. Di Oliver, Mrs. Maisie Ormiston, Mrs. Isobel Russell, Mrs. Alison Seeley, Mrs. Margaret N. Shields, Mrs. Norma Shiels, Mrs. Marjory Stewart, Mrs. Myra Tait, the late Miss. Christina Turnbull and Mrs. Cathie Whillans; also to Messrs. Findlay Adam, James Anderson, Robert Armstrong MBE, Neil Corbett, Alan Graham, Roger Hart, William Jardine, Jason Marshall, James Matthews, Ian A. Scott, David Stewart, Jake Thomson, James Thomson, John Walsh and Dennis Whitehead. I thank them also for assistance in identifying many of the people in the photographs and for discussing with me their knowledge of them in relation to the Opera.

I have also been fortunate to benefit from the assistance and advice of Miss. Lesley Fraser, Mrs. Mona Hope, District Registrar, Miss. Zilla Oddy of Hawick Heritage Hub and Mrs. Betty Warwick; also Messrs. Ian Fraser, Billy Hamilton, David A. Hill, Ian W. Landles, Derek Lunn, Allan McCredie, Leslie Mitchell, David Morrison and Brian Walker together with the staff of the Scottish Borders Council Museums Service and the staff of Hawick Public Library. Finally, my thanks to the office bearers of HAOS for inviting me to undertake this project, and to my wife, Alison, for casting a critical and informed eye over the text.

Ian W. Seeley, Hawick, 2010

CONTENTS

Chapter I

BEGINNERS, PLEASE

The first secretarial minute of Hawick Amateur Operatic Society (HAOS) records -

"Public Library Buildings, Hawick, 15th November, 1910. A meeting called by advertisement, of ladies and gentlemen interested in the formation of an Operatic Society was held tonight at the above address."

So was born an institution which, for a century, has remained central to Hawick`s entertainment calendar, known affectionately as `The Opera`.

The advertisement to which they had responded appeared in the local Press on 11th November, 1910, having itself been agreed upon at an informal preliminary meeting in the back shop of John Hume, hatter and hosier, 57 High Street.

The meeting of 15th November confirmed the following office bearers to administer the affairs of the Society; John Hume, President; Robert Rimmer (Sax-Horn Bandmaster), Vice-President and Musical Director; George Reekie (hairdresser) and James Stewart (Co-Operative shop assistant), Joint Secretaries; and Matthew Scott (tweed merchant), Treasurer. A further notice appeared in the local Press on 18th November, exhorting intending members to present themselves for enrolment in the Public Library Committee Room on Monday, 21st November.

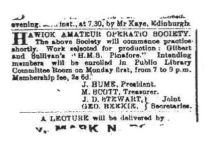

Such was the response that rehearsals for the first production, Gilbert and Sullivan`s *HMS Pinafore*, commenced without delay under Robert Rimmer`s direction. For some commentators it evoked a sense of *déjà vu* because this was not Hawick`s first such venture. So, while Hawick Amateur Operatic Society is not the oldest of the Border societies, it might have been, had the body styling itself Hawick Amateur Opera Company (HAOC) survived.

HAWICK AMATEUR OPERA COMPANY (HAOC)

This company, formed in 1897, by the organist of Wilton Church, Walter Fiddes Wilson (1861-1925), largely from its choir and that of St. John`s Church where he had held a similar position from 1880 to 1891, produced only two shows. *Patience,* by Gilbert and Sullivan, was presented in the Large Hall of the Exchange over the New Year holiday period of 1897/98 and *The Gondoliers* just over a year later in January, 1899 at the same venue (now the location of Hawick Heritage Hub). Fiddes Wilson was Musical Director and his friend and fellow manufacturer James Boyd Sime (1865-1953), of Sime and Williamson, `Stage Director` (Producer).

Walter Fiddes Wilson (1861-1925)

Of *Patience* the *Hawick News* observed -

> "The opera was very well staged, and the attention given
> to the costumier`s department showed that neither pains
> nor expense had been spared in giving due effect to the
> spectacular aspects of the performance."

In the case of *The Gondoliers* it was a little more critical -

> "The present venture cannot be said to have attained the
> all-round degree of merit which marked their initial effort.
> It was on the whole more `amateurish` but still achieved
> sufficient distinction to ensure complete enjoyment on the
> part of the audience."

No punches pulled, then, on the part of the critic, but this is important because it allows us to gauge a conception of standard, and it should be noted that *The Gondoliers* had, among its ranks, some very noteworthy Hawick musicians – Fiddes Wilson himself, Adam Grant of Hawick song renown, the Bell brothers from St. John`s – Henry, William and the legendary tenor John (for whom Grant was to write *Up Wi` Auld Hawick* in 1902). James Boyd Sime would become conductor of Hawick Amateur Musical and Dramatic Society which (had the First World War not intervened) could have presented a fatal challenge to the fledgling Hawick Amateur Operatic Society (HAOS).[1]

---

[1] The *Hawick Advertiser* 30/11/1914 reported their `largely attended meeting` in the Public Library Hall on 27/1/1914 when` it was decided to proceed with the rehearsal of `A Country Girl` and a committee was appointed to further the work of the Society`. Not until 1915 were practices advertised for 25/1/ 1915 and 12/2/1915, but as the War progressed this society and its aspirations faded into oblivion.

Also present in the cast was tenor James Sutherland of the Imperial Hotel (Cornet of 1901 and elder brother of Scottish rugby internationalist Wattie Sutherland). Sutherland was one of only three stage performers of Hawick Amateur Opera Company who would return to the boards with Hawick Amateur Operatic Society in the twentieth century. The others were John H. Young, draper, and Richard Lillico, tobacconist. Sutherland and Young lasted only one year with the new Society, the former finding outlet for his fine tenor voice at Common Riding-related events. Lillico did not join HAOS until 1919. John Bell, lauded by *Hawick News* as one who `rose greatly above the general level` with his rendition of *Take A Pair Of Sparkling Eyes*, was never to know at first hand anything of the new HAOS. He left Hawick for Edinburgh in 1909 to work for Scottish Motor Traction.

Tom Henderson (the future Sir Thomas) as Guiseppe (seated) with John Bell as Marco
in the HAOC production of *The Gondoliers* in the Exchange, January, 1899.

This digression into Hawick Amateur Opera Company (HAOC) of 1897-99 begs the question of its demise and the lessons it held for the new Hawick Amateur Operatic Society (HAOS) in 1910. HAOC failed because it was not really a company in the administrative sense. It was, in most respects, an *ad hoc* group of `invited friends` (mainly of the professional and business-owning variety) and very much the brainchild of one man – Walter Fiddes Wilson. To the great and good already mentioned in the production of *The Gondoliers* may be added the name of Thomas H. Armstrong of Ardenlea, solicitor and Session Clerk of Wilton Church as The Duke of Plaza-Toro.

It is not known why Fiddes Wilson called a halt in 1899 because he continued to exert considerable musical influence in Hawick over the following two decades. He may have taken a `scunner` at the *Hawick News* report and decided enough was enough. Who knows? The problem was that with no constitution, no properly elected officials, no committee and no stated aims, there was, administratively, no company and no independent structure, or impetus to replace Wilson when he lost interest. And so, what was essentially a `first` for Hawick and the Borders was, over the following decade, blurred from public memory.

Chapter II

CURTAIN UP

HMS Pinafore and the pre-Great War Shows

It is perhaps surprising that, of the officials elected at Hawick Amateur Operatic Society`s first meeting on 15th November, 1910, only one, Matthew Scott (Treasurer) was a playing member. The new Society would, in the first instance, be steered by individuals well accustomed to dealing with the public. It would be democratic and meritocratic in its outlook. Producers, musical directors, local Carusos and divas might come and go but the democratic administrative structure should, ideally, ensure the survival of the Society provided, of course, that membership could be attracted and sustained and that financial and performance issues could be addressed successfully.(In the old HAOC, Fiddes Wilson and Boyd Sime had underwritten the enterprise from their own pockets). The availability and limitations of rehearsal and performance accommodation (halls, stages, dressing room facilities, etc.) would dog HAOS for the greater part of its existence.

The choice of *HMS Pinafore* for the debut of HAOS will be well understood by operetta enthusiasts. It contains straightforward, well-written choruses, very manageable solos, duets and a very attractive trio - `*Never Mind The Why and Wherefore*`. The leading lady, Josephine, is afforded a single, but conspicuous show-piece in `*A Simple Sailor*`. The whole work is modest, exuding Victorian charm, yet sufficiently daft to produce unmitigated glee; good clean fun, in fact. In 1910, much of its music was, even in those days before national radio, familiar to the public. Hawick Sax-Horn Band, since 1879, had been offering selections from *HMS Pinafore* in its regular band-stand programmes.

Robert Rimmer set about his work and, once the musical content had, in his judgment, reached the required standard, the Society sought the services of a `dramatic coach`. This was to be John Sutherland Brewster, an Edinburgh solicitor`s clerk and a member of that city's Southern Light Opera Company with a passion for Gilbert and Sullivan. It was to be an association with HAOS which would last for almost a quarter of a century, his final production for the Society being *The Mikado* of 1934.

Robert Rimmer (1863-1934)
First Musical Director

John S. Brewster (1878-1956)
First Producer

On ...
Speaker : MR TOM ...
ATTRACTIVE PROGRAMME.
Tickets to be had from Members of Committee.

NEW THEATRE, HAWICK.

GRAND PRODUCTION OF Messrs GILBERT
& SULLIVAN'S COMIC OPERA,

"H.M.S. PINAFORE,"

Or "The Lass that Loved a Sailor."
(By kind permission of Mrs D'Oyly Carte).
BY THE
HAWICK AMATEUR OPERATIC SOCIETY,
under the distinguished patronage of
Provost, Magistrates, and Town Council of Hawick.
Proceeds solely in aid of Local Charities.
Four Nights—MARCH 29th, 30th, 31st,
and APRIL 1st.

DRAMATIS PERSONÆ:
The Right Hon. Sir Jos. Porter, K.C.B.
(First Lord of the Admiralty) Mr ROBERT WILSON
Captain Corcoran (Commanding "H.M.S.
Pinafore") ... ... Mr JOHN H. YOUNG
Ralph Rackstraw (Able Seaman)
Mr JAMES SUTHERLAND
Dick Deadeye (Able Seaman) ... Mr W. P. GAYLOR
Bill Bobstay (Botswain's Mate) Mr J. D. LUCE
Bob Beckett (Carpenter's Mate) Mr WM. HARDIE
Midshipmite ... ... Master H. P. BISHER
Josephine ... ... Mrs RIMMER
Hebe (Sir Joseph's First Cousin) Miss ETTA GUY
Little Buttercup (A Portsmouth Bumboat
Woman) ... ... Miss M. O. SCOTT
Chorus of Sailors, Marines, Orchestra of 18
Performers.
Conductor and Musical Director—MR R. RIMMER.
Admission—Dress Circle (numbered and reserved),
3s ; Orchestra Stalls (numbered and reserved), 2s 6d ;
Pit Stalls, 2s ; Pit, 1s ; Gallery 6d.
Booking Plans at Mr Grant's, Music Warehouse,
Bridge Street.
Doors open, 7.30. Commence at 8 p.m.
Carriages at 10.15.
Early door to ticket-holders only at 7 o'clock.
Tickets may be had at the shops of Mr Hume,
hatter, High Street ; Messrs Wilson and Bain,
chemists, Oliver Place and 12 Sandbed ; Mr Reekie,
hairdresser, High Street ; and from members of the
Company. G. M. REEKIE, Secy.

delivery at
later than tw
1911, of a no'
date, or by
date was not
Officer.†
7. The
Division, at
the Polling
seventh day
Each vote
property in
situate, and
in any one
it is situate
8. The
till eigh
9. T'
10.
be m
Tak

Da

Roy
* Nor.

† Notic

HAK

baths ;
day.—M

Consul
By Ir

(

Brewster had his work cut out. By all accounts, the talent, though musically accomplished, was, in dramatics, `raw`. But Brewster was more than equal to the task, and *HMS Pinafore* was rapturously applauded over its four night run, 29th March to 1st April, 1911 in the Croft Road, or New Theatre (affectionately remembered in Hawick as the `Wee Thea`).[2]

---

[2] The Salvation Army citadel now occupies the site of the `Wee Thea`, which was destroyed by fire in 1955.

The Cast of *HMS Pinafore* at the end of the final performance, 1ˢᵗ April, 1911 (note the bouquets)

Principals - James D.	Etta	Robert	Edith	James	M.O.	John H.	William P.
Luck	Guy	Wilson	Rimmer	Sutherland	Scott	Young	Gaylor
(Bill Bobstay)	(Hebe)	(Sir Joseph)	(Josephine)	(Ralph)	(Buttercup)	(Captain)	(Dick Deadeye)

Ellen Charters, mother of recent Producer Jean Wintrope, is the lady in white behind the squatting bearded sailor (centre)

A beacon had been lit in Hawick – one which was kindled in the hearts and minds of Teries. `The Opera` would become enmeshed in the very fabric of Hawick. That cross-fertilisation of recreational interest which so marks an intimate community was evident from the start. The `credits` page of the first programme reveals family connections which would bind the Society through the twentieth century. There are the Gladstone sisters, Jean, and Lizzie who found romance and married James Howarth from the `Gentlemen`s Chorus`. Two sons, Walter and George and a daughter Betty from that marriage would be prominent on `The Opera` stage after the Second World War. Betty carved a niche for herself in comedy roles. Adam Aitken, partner in the engineering firm of Turnbull and Aitken, was followed into the Society by son George and daughters Nancy, Mary, and Jessie (Cissie). George was in from 1920 as a child, being the Midshipmite in *HMS Pinafore* (1920) and Nancy was the Society`s Secretary from 1965 to 1980 after appearing in all the post-War shows to 1963. Ellen Charters, of the Ladies` Chorus, was to nurture her own operatic dynasty with daughters Nan and Jane (Jean) Whillans (later Mrs. Kenneth Ellis and Mrs. Neil Wintrope respectively) – and not forgetting son Jim, who carried The Lord High Executioner`s sword in 1934!

---

[3] It became standard practice, between the Wars, for Hawick Common-Riding Committee to invite principals from the Society`s show in a particular year, to grace the Town Hall stage for this important function. This practice has fallen away over the past fifty years.

So, the Opera became indelibly associated with certain families (as with Hawick Common-Riding) while simultaneously welcoming new blood and developing cross-community bonds. Bill Gaylor, optician, for example, (Deadeye of 1911) was `Mr Hawick`, singing at every Colour Bussing Ceremony of the Common-Riding between 1912 and 1960; John H. Young, draper, and Ex-Cornet Sutherland (Captain Corcoran and Ralph respectively) were also frequent entertainers at these ceremonies;[3] John Ballantyne (Bass Chorus) became the Cornet`s Acting Father in 1935 and President of Hawick Rugby Club 1955-57: Etta Guy (Hebe) was Cornet Elder`s Lass in 1913; Robert Wilson (Sir Joseph Porter, KCB) rose to become chairman and chief executive of Hawick`s largest pre-War knitwear firm, Innes, Henderson & Co.; and John Campbell (of the orchestra of 1911) became joint managing director of one of the town`s leading tweed producers, Blenkhorn and Richardson.

HAWICK AMATEUR OPERATIC SOCIETY

PRESENT THEIR FIRST PRODUCTION

" H.M.S. PINAFORE "

A Musical Play by W. S. Gilbert and A. Sullivan

In The Theatre, Hawick

From 29th March to 1st April, 1911

DRAMATIS PERSONÆ

Rt. Hon. Sir JOS. PORTER, K.C.B.	ROBERT WILSON
CAPTAIN CORCORAN	JOHN H. YOUNG
RALPH RACKSTRAW	JAS. SUTHERLAND
DICK DEADEYE	W. P. GAYLOR
BILL BOBSTAY	J. D. LUCK
BOB BECKETT	Wm. HARDIE
MIDSHIPMITE	Master H. P. BISHER
JOSEPHINE	Mrs RIMMER
HEBE	Miss ETTA GUY
LITTLE BUTTERCUP	Miss M. O. SCOTT

LADIES' CHORUS : SOPRANOS—Misses Lizzie Gladstone, Jean Gladstone, Mary White, Sarah Armstrong, Annie Tait, Ina Turnbull, Lizzie Taylor, Ada Tait, Ellen Charters, Agnes Stewart.

CONTRALTOS—Misses Bessie Henderson, Jessie Miller, Beatrice Miller, Bella Miller, Bella Murray, Molly Scott, Jean Milligan.

GENTLEMEN'S CHORUS : TENORS—Messrs J. Anderson, Joe Turnbull, Wr. Turnbull, W. Scott, J. Howarth, G. Kyle.

BASSES—Messrs J. Wilson, J. Inglis, M. Scott, A. Aitken, J. Ballantyne, R. Williamson.

MARINES—Mr D. S. McBean (Sergeant), Messrs J. Glendinning, J. Campbell, J. Rae.

CONDUCTOR—Mr Rimmer.

ORCHESTRA : 1st VIOLINS—Messrs J. D. Swinton, J. S. Imrie, J. Campbell, Miss M. McVittie.

2nd VIOLINS—Mr J. Elliot, Misses B. Scott and E. D. Hunter.

CELLO—Mr Beaumont Taylor. BASS—Mr J. C. Ball. FLUTE—Mr J. Anderson. CLARINET—Mr W. Ballantyne. HORN—Mr W. Moyes. CORNETS—Messrs W. Riddle and G. B. Douglas. TROMBONE—Mr A. Beattie. DRUMS—Mr A. Anderson. PIANO—Mr Wm. Campbell.

PHOTOS AND MAKE-UP—Mr J. E. D. Murray.

Wilson held the presidency of the Society from 1911 to 1928, Campbell succeeding him thereafter until 1950. Both were highly respected, not only for their success in the workplace, but for their outstanding performing talent on stage. It is in the nature of Hawick that it was no problem for a mill chief executive to share the stage with his workers in a similar fashion to what might occur on a Hawick rugby field or in Common-Riding circles. This was, and is, Hawick and this was Hawick`s very own Operatic Society – the warp and weft of the community.

HMS Pinafore was adjudged an outstanding success. At the first Annual General Meeting of the Society in the Public Library Committee Room on 7th April, 1911, the interim President, William E. Wilson, was voluble in his praise, intimating that a financial surplus of £30 was available for donation to charities. From its inception, charitable donation was a cardinal principle of the Society`s ethos.

This meeting was key to how the Society would develop because on that evening the presidency changed hands, Robert Wilson replacing William E. Wilson.[4] Robert Wilson (1882-1964) was a remarkable man – `self-made` from very modest beginnings in a family of stocking makers and hand-frame knitters, a rising star in the knitwear industry, a committed socialist, devotee of Esperanto, a future town councillor and J.P., a self-confessed spiritualist and a passionate Savoyard. He adored the works of Gilbert and Sullivan and resolutely avoided investing his considerable stage talent in musicals.[5]

For the following three years up to the Great War, Wilson gathered together a strong administrative team to run the Opera. Its members were, of course, elected, but it was fortuitous that they were people whose Thespian passion burned as did his own. Most notable among them was William D. Turnbull (1879-1965)[6] who was elected Treasurer in 1913 and remained so until 1932. Turnbull was indefatigable in his service to the Society, being a playing member until 1933 then serving on the Committee until 1938. After the Second World War, he served as honorary auditor until his death in 1965.

Robert Wilson (1882-1964)   William D. Turnbull (1879-1965)

Turnbull was the kind of man Wilson enjoyed working with – utterly dependable, utterly dedicated; someone willing, if so required, to serve year in and year out in whatever capacity. Wilson`s `dream team`, the men who made the Opera, would not be complete until after the Great War.

---

[4] William Elliot Wilson (1868-1950), chemist, had replaced John Hume who had resigned after only a few weeks as President. Wilson was a very active force in Hawick Archaeological Society, of which he was Vice-President for many years before becoming their President 1945-50.
[5] Robert Wilson`s last stage appearance for HAOS was as Major General Stanley in *The Pirates of Penzance* in December, 1926. He took no part in the Society`s first musical, *The Nautch Girl,* staged in March that year and he resigned as President in 1928. He was subsequently elected Honorary President. He is often referred to as Wilson of Wellfield, this being his home between the wars. The site of Wellfield House and its policies is now occupied by Wilton Primary School.
[6] William D. Turnbull was in business as a director of The Crescent Cleaning Co. in Bridge Street.

The show chosen for 1912 was *The Pirates of Penzance*, the venue once again the Croft Road Theatre – a happy arrangement for a fledgling society because it was purpose-built for stage presentation – "the cosy and well-appointed theatre of which Hawick folks are justly proud" as described in *The Hawick Advertiser* (31/3/1914). W. Payne Seddon, the lessee of the theatre, was sympathetic to the aims of the new Society and arranged for his own scenic artist, Mr. George Collier of Hull, to build and paint the scenery. The *Hawick News* (15/3/1912) duly observed –

> "They are not the slap-dash order of scenery, but are carefully-executed works of art, highly creditable to the artist and Theatre."

But there were problems, as the outstanding success of *The Pirates* demonstrated. The `Wee Thea` was going to be too small for the burgeoning Opera audiences. Other issues were looming, principal among which was the spectacular rise in popularity of the cinema. This would see the theatre facility develop as a `picture palace` presenting `a few of the best dramatic companies` and `pictures, but the very best procurable`. For HAOS, however, seating capacity, balancing the books relative to ticket price and, from 1916, the Entertainment Tax, were issues to be addressed.

For *The Pirates of Penzance* the number of playing members increased by two to forty four. The orchestra remained at the standard D`Oyly Carte package of sixteen for amateur orchestras plus pianist. New arrivals were William D. Turnbull to the bass chorus and Jessie E. Murray to the contraltos. She was a machinist in the Peter Scott factory and a singer of some note locally.[7] The principals in *Pirates* were little changed from those in *Pinafore*; Robert Wilson as the *Modern Major General*, Bill Gaylor as the Pirate King, Mrs. Edith Rimmer as Mabel, William Hardie as the Sergeant of Police, Miss M.O. Scott as Ruth, the pirate maid, with new arrival Adam Leithead as Frederick. Safe play, then, but understandable in a new enterprise.

William P. Gaylor as the Pirate King –
The Pirates Of Penzance 1912

The Society`s second AGM on 22nd March, 1912 confirmed a surplus of £15 to be distributed

---

[7] In October, 1914 Jessie Easton Murray married Adam Grant`s younger son George. Grant and J.E.D. Murray (no relation) wrote *The Wail of Flodden* for her part (Ailie) in the Hawick Quater-Centenary Pageant of 1914. She sang at the Colour Bussing of 1919 but, within a year, she and George were citizens of Niagara Falls, Canada. She made a return trip to Hawick with her 14 year-old son, `Master Adam Grant` in the summer of 1936, giving solos, etc. in St. John`s Church. Her father-in-law, Adam, retired as organist there 28/6/1936 after 45 years in post, which event may have resulted in the visit. Jessie died in 1976 aged 85.

equally among the Cottage Hospital, Jubilee Nurses and the Scottish Society for the Prevention of Cruelty to Children. It also confirmed James D.Luck and George A. Kyle as joint Secretaries resulting from George Reekie`s emigration to Australia. *The Mikado* was agreed upon as the next production and, in a never-to-be-repeated gesture, Hawick Town Council granted free use of the Town Hall for the production. After considered assessment of possible audience projections in the larger auditorium, it was decided to reduce the number of performances from four to three.

But there was a price of a different kind to pay. Gone were the purpose-designed facilities of the `Wee Thea`; gone was the `cosiness` and comfortable seating. What the Society got was a draughty hall, cramped stage, pew-like long benches in the galleries and moveable wooden chairs in the area – and no appreciable changes would come until the mid - nineteen sixties! The Town Hall would continue to present problems for societies like the Opera. (Hawick Choral Society was in the same boat). It does still. In 1912, however, it appeared the only positive option available and the Society accepted the Council`s largesse with open arms.

The Mikado played in the Town Hall on 27th, 28th February and 1st March, 1913 to `crowded houses`. There was a noticeable change in the choice of principals, apart from Bill Gaylor as Ko-Ko, the Lord High Executioner (he had been Dick Deadeye in *Pinafore* and the Pirate King in 1912). The `new` principals were John Campbell, William D. Turnbull, John Kirsopp, George A. Kyle, Bella Haig and Jessie E. Murray. Campbell, who took the role of Pooh Bah, was a trained bass who, in Edwardian times, had regularly taken solo parts in Hawick Choral Society`s annual oratorio performances. The local Press reported that "Mr. Gaylor added to his already enviable reputation among play-goers" and "Miss. J. E. Murray..... scored brilliantly (as Katisha). Her acting was dramatic and at the end of the first act, she fairly brought down the house.......she has firmly established her reputation." A week later, the *Hawick Express* reported the close of the Saturday night performance when –

> "Misses. Haig, Gladstone and Armstrong (*Three Little Maids)* received beautiful bouquets, while Miss. J.E. Murray, who had so ably played `Katisha`, was the recipient of numerous floral tributes."

Mention of Jean Gladstone and Sarah Armstrong serves to highlight the vital contribution made to operatic societies everywhere by those true stalwarts who seldom get the starring role but who are awarded minor, but nonetheless important parts in the general scheme of things. They flit in and out of the chorus over years of loyal support.

Sarah Armstrong and Jean Gladstone participated in every show, bar one each, to1938. That record has been eclipsed by a few of the present members of the Society, but they are a breed which is seldom fully appreciated by those who take centre stage. They are the sinews of any amateur operatic society. They don`t contrive to stay away when there is `no part for them`.

Jessie E. Murray as Katisha
The Mikado 1913

William D. Turnbull as
the Mikado 1913

Sarah Armstrong as Peep Bo
The Mikado 1913

John Kirsopp as Nanki Poo
The Mikado 1913

Like William D. Turnbull, they support the society through thick and thin. Robert Wilson, as President, set an example in 1913, joining the chorus of *The Mikado*, singing alongside the Society's first pianist, William Campbell and newcomer Robert Carlyle Wilson – names destined to reverberate through HAOS after the Great War and, in Campbell's case, even after the Second World War.

The `Piv` and *Iolanthe*

On 10th November, 1913, Provost Melrose, at the invitation of the owners, officially opened ` Scott's Pavilion Theatre of Pictures and Varieties`, which Teries soon dubbed `The Piv`. With comfortable seating and a large stage to accommodate the `varieties` component of its title, the temptation was just too great for the office-bearers of HAOS. *Iolanthe* was the show chosen at the Society's AGM on 11th March, 1913 for the coming season and, almost immediately, Robert Wilson and his new Treasurer, William D. Turnbull, began negotiating with a very sympathetic Mr. Scott. The show was advertised for the Pavilion on 6th March, 1914 as a `GRAND PRODUCTION BY HAWICK AMATEUR OPERATIC SOCIETY of "*Iolanthe*" with Full Chorus and Orchestra of 60 Performers`.

And so it came to pass. *Iolanthe* was presented in the Pavilion Theatre for `4 Nights Only` commencing on 11th March, 1914. The *Hawick Express* of 20th March noted that the concluding performance was given before `a crowded and enthusiastic audience.` It continued –

> "Encores were frequent and hearty and the principals were the recipients of several handsome `favours`. At the close, Mr. Robert Wilson, President of the Society, thanked the public for their hearty and generous support and acknowledged the splendid services of Mr. Rimmer."

This was Robert Rimmer's swan song in Hawick. Early in 1914 he had been appointed Bandmaster to Dunikier Colliery Band in Kirkcaldy where he lived until his death in 1934. His progeny were to form one of the most distinguished banding dynasties in Britain. It was typical of Rimmer's rectitude that, despite his earlier appointment to Kirkcaldy, he honoured his commitment to HAOS. He and Mrs. Rimmer were the recipients of generous gifts from the Society following the final performance of *Iolanthe*.

It was the end of an era, although few, if any, realised it. Having chosen the coming season's show (*Patience*) at their AGM in St. Mary's Hall on 27th March, 1914, the Society endeavoured to secure the services of Mr. Harry Bower (Rimmer's replacement as Sax-Horn Bandmaster) as Musical Director. As things turned out, neither would materialise. *Iolanthe* came to symbolise a bygone world, some kind of Arcadian dream, as Europe blew itself apart on 4th August, 1914. With many of the men enlisting for service, any hope of staging *Patience* slowly vanished. John Campbell enlisted with the Field Artillery; John Ballantyne saw service with the KOSB at Gallipoli; Bill Gaylor went to the RAMC; and so the drip,

The Cast of *Iolanthe* after the final performance on 14th March, 1914

Principals – left to right (seated) – Jean Gladstone (Fleta), Walter Turnbull (Earl Tolloller), Agnes Stewart (Celia),
John Campbell (Strephon), Bella Gray (Phyllis), Robert Rimmer (Conductor), Mary Armstrong (Iolanthe),
William P. Gaylor (Lord Chancellor), Jessie E. Murray (Fairy Queen), William Hardie (Private Willis),
Lizzie Taylor (Leila), James M. Wilson (Earl of Mountararat)

drip of male personnel continued. Because HAOS was a `young` society (the majority of its members were under thirty five in 1914), it was vulnerable. The Society presented a `Grand Concert and Entertainment` in the Pavilion Theatre on the 14th February, 1915 in aid of the Red Cross, but the introduction of conscription in 1916 was the *coup de grâce* and it fell into abeyance. Two members were lost to the War – David Houliston and Thomas Turnbull. Given the scale of the carnage, perhaps this was a lesser toll from its ranks than the Society might have expected, but nevertheless a tragedy for their families, and there were many in the Opera who also lost loved ones.

John Campbell as Strephon
Iolanthe 1914

Walter Turnbull as Earl Tolloller
Iolanthe 1914

Chapter III

THE INTER-WAR YEARS (1)

The `Twenties

Following an exploratory meeting in the Public Library on 22nd September, 1919 to consider the future of the Society, its existing members present concluded that there were still sufficient numbers of former active members and of intending new members of promising ability to warrant the Society`s embracing a work for the coming season. The most favourable course of action, it was suggested, would be to take up *HMS Pinafore.* There was a certain symbolism in the choice of the work that had launched the Society almost a decade earlier. This was a renaissance if not exactly a new beginning, a second chance to establish a dynamic society, and they had the benefit of past experience to assist them. Robert Wilson was re-confirmed as President with William D. Turnbull as Treasurer, and (to Wilson`s delight) Adam M. Aitken agreed to take on the onerous task of Secretary.

Wilson`s natural flair for business promotion presupposed a wider vision of what HAOS was about. He saw the Society not merely as an association which put on an annual show, but also as a potential engine for the promotion of culture generally and, four months to the day after that exploratory meeting, the Scottish Orchestra appeared in Hawick Town Hall on 22nd January, 1920 – "Under the auspices of The Hawick Amateur Operatic Society." And this would not be a `one-off`.[8]

John Campbell (1880-1950)

Adam M. Aitken (1889-1971)

William Campbell (1884-1956)

Some might have considered this folly, especially as the Society had still to present its own show, with no funds in the kitty; but it was typical of Wilson`s charismatic leadership that he saw in it prestigious publicity for the Society. Aitken, also a founder member, was in perfect agreement. The administration of the scheme fell to him and he was masterly in its execution. An overwhelming success, the message to the public was clear – `You ain`t seen nothin` yet! The Society is up and running; now come and support us.`

The Musical Director and Conductor for the revival of *HMS Pinafore* (and the Society) was not Harry Bower, but the Society`s very first pianist, William Campbell, younger brother of bass soloist John[9]. A cashier with Wilson and Glenny, tweedmakers, he was organist and choirmaster of East Bank Church. A highly respected and popular musician, he was to wield

---

[8] They returned in the same year, under similar arrangements, giving concerts in the Town Hall on 22nd and 23rd December, 1920. Wilson persevered with this policy, bringing the Arts League of Service to the town in November, 1922 when, along with a programme of music and dance, they presented Shaw`s *Arms And The Man*, all under the aegis of HAOS.

[9] They were members of a family who came to Hawick from Walkerburn in the early 1880s and set up a drapery at 6 Howegate (R. & J. Campbell). Towards the end of 1933, John Campbell brought out two records of the Hawick songs.

the conductor`s baton for the following thirty years and, after that, continue as chorus master for a further three. The Society`s pianist for the following fourteen years was Charles Eustace Davidson, son of a local doctor. Stability, consolidation and enterprise were the watchwords of the resuscitated HAOS. For a decade from its revival, the Society remained (with one important exception in 1926) thirled to presenting the works of Gilbert and Sullivan.

HMS Pinafore 1920

A violent storm heralded the revival of *HMS Pinafore* in (despite all the misgivings) the Town Hall on 17th March, 1920. The hall, though not packed, was well filled. The *Hawick Express* (19/3/1920) reported –

> "The weather was of the stormiest description, so much so that the wind and rain driving with hurricane violence on the roof of the building proved something of a distraction at times.. The parts allotted to the young lady principals were not rendered easier.....where an additional strain was put on them....amid the noise of the storm raging without."

Fifty two members took the stage. Notable new principals were Robert Carlyle Wilson (tenor) as Ralph, Peggy Davidson[10] as Josephine and Ada Henderson as Buttercup. Robert Carlyle Wilson (1892-1971), who took the part of Ralph, became the Opera`s favourite tenor of the `twenties.

Part of the Cast of *HMS Pinafore*, March, 1920

Not many can be identified accurately, but the Midshipmite is George Aitken. His father, Adam, is in the centre of the row behind him. David Stothart is 3rd from the right in the front row; William Whillans 4th from the left and Tom Shortreed 4th from the right in the middle row. Belle Millar (later Mrs. T. Hamilton of Earlside) is 2nd from the right in the middle row.

---

[10] Cornet`s Lass to Tom Winning, 1919.

Among the surge of new members making their operatic debuts in 1920 were Thomas E. Shortreed, David O. Stothart, William J. Whillans, Peggy Hunter, Belle Millar and Florence McKie. The three men all became office bearers of the long tradition, who sustained the Society beyond the Second World War, Shortreed eventually becoming Treasurer (1933-58) and Whillans[11] `Production Secretary` then Secretary (1936-1956). Here again, it is worth restating that a society thrives and survives not only by the favours of its `stars` but on the members who are in it for the long haul.

In *Pinafore,* John Campbell continued his development as a much-admired bass soloist throughout the `twenties and the first half of the `thirties. He became one of Wilson`s `dream team` when he was elected Vice-President in 1921. This society, one would think, could hardly fail. The decade which began with *Pinafore* Mark Two saw the debuts of other notables – Norman Henderson, John Johnstone and Greta Warwick (1921); Robert Baxter and Tom Cowan Scott (1922), Agnes Young (1925); Nainie Farries (1926); Maimie B. Clark and William Pickthall (1928); and Margaret D. McKie, younger sister of Flo, (1929).

Robert Wilson – Sir Joseph Porter
HMS Pinafore 1920

John Campbell – Captain Corcoran
HMS Pinafore 1920

---

[11] William James Whillans (1889-1961) joined the Society in 1914 after *Iolanthe.* He married founder member Helen (Ellen) Charters in September 1919. A hosiery foreman with the Peter Scott company, he was Secretary of HAOS 1936-1956. He was also Secretary of Hawick Horticultural Society and was greatly involved with the Vertish Hill Sports of which he was `Captain of the Ring.`

In the tradition of long service to the Opera it would be churlish to omit mention of Richard More, violinist, who came down from Edinburgh every Spring from 1929 to 1960 (War years excepted) to lead the Opera orchestra. His was a familiar face to many Teries of a bygone, more genteel age, who recognised him as one of the musicians who played in the restaurant of Patrick Thomson`s department store on Edinburgh`s `Bridges`.[12] This, in itself, says something about the ambience generated in the Society, but it is a fact that players on the stage don`t always appreciate what they owe to the people in dark attire in front of the proscenium. In a similar vein, the contribution of Hawick`s own J.E.D. Murray[13] in the make-up department cannot be overlooked. A keen amateur dramatist and playwright himself, he performed this service for HAOS from its inception in 1910 until

1935. He had also done this for the short-lived HAOC in Victorian times. His photography is responsible for many of the images presented with this text.

Despite Robert Wilson`s aspirations for the Society as a matrix for the Arts in general, these had to be balanced against its well-being and *raison d`être* – namely (in the words of its own advertisement of 8/4/1921) "to continue putting before its many patrons clean and wholesome entertainments". Patronage and donation to charity were laudable and creditworthy aims but they did not assist in balancing the books, a fact conceded in the Society`s advertisement for an extra night of *Patience* (1921). This may be seen as presaging the Patrons` List of 1926.

The Attraction of the Musical

As the `twenties progressed, so did the desire to finally lay that old pre-Great War era to rest. The war had swept away so much; nothing was ever going to be the same again. The horror of the conflict, and the grim post-War economic realities which resulted in the General Strike of 1926 and the Great Depression which followed brought a craving for escapism and romance which was fuelled by the massive popularity of the cinema. The artificiality and caricature-obsessed works of Gilbert and Sullivan now seemed distinctly *passé* and, as a result, there was increasing pressure within amateur societies to adopt the musical play, or musical, rather than operetta, as the basis for future development. But it was not an easy move for HAOS,

---

[12] In 1951 and 1952 More took over the Conductor`s baton from an ailing Willie Campbell, conscripting his brother Albert into the orchestra in his place.
[13] John Edward Dodd Murray (1858-1936), photographer, poet, playwright, was Cornet of Hawick in 1890 and Cornet`s Acting Father on four subsequent occasions; 1901 (J. Sutherland), 1905 (W.E. Kyle), 1912 (J.D. Bonsor) and 1925 (G.D. Scott).

and one which resulted in there being no HAOS show in 1927.[14]

The Officers of the Dragoon Guards – *Patience* 1921

BACK – Robert Baxter, Norman C. Henderson, John Johnstone, Walter Corbett, W. Rutherford, ?,
FRONT – Richard Lillico, Tom A. Shearman, William D. Turnbull, David C. Scott,[15] Frank Gray

From 1920 to 1925 inclusive, the Society mounted productions of *Pinafore*, *Patience*, *The Gondoliers*, *The Mikado*, *The Yeomen Of The Guard*, and *Iolanthe*. The old stagers – Aitken, Campbell, Gaylor, Turnbull and Wilson were still there. The new solo `discoveries` were Robert Baxter, John Johnstone, Robert Carlyle Wilson, William J. Whillans, Belle Millar, Peggy Hunter, Flo McKie, Greta Warwick and Agnes Young, a niece of J.E.D. Murray.[16] Agnes Young was destined to become one of the Society`s unquestionably outstanding leading ladies and, arguably, the most accomplished lady vocalist in its history.

Following the AGM in 1925, however, it was reported that " ....the selection of a work to be produced next session was delayed pending further consideration". In due course a practice for all members was announced for Monday, 17th June, 1925 in the Constitutional (Conservative) Club Hall at 8 p.m. The Society had chosen to take a chance on musical comedy and opted for what now seems a corny show – *The Nautch Girl* (from an Indian dancing girl troupe). Its very subtitle, *The Rajah of Chutneypore* and characters such as Baboo Currie (taken by Robert Baxter) perhaps give a clue to its potential impact.

---

[14] The list of past productions which appears annually in HAOS programmes perpetuates a `white lie`. *The Pirates of Penzance,* listed for 1927, actually took place in the Town Hall, 7th-11th December, 1926.
[15] David C. Scott, Sandbed – butcher, was the brother of Cornet Bert Scott (1947) and grandfather of Cornet Rory Culton (1993).
[16] Agnes Young`s father, master baker of the Sandbed, Alex. Young, was a brother of J.E.D. Murray`s wife Margaret (`Daisy`).

Margaret (Peggy) Davidson) as Patience,
1921. Cornet's Lass 1919

William P. Gaylor
as the Lord High Executioner, Ko Ko
– *The Mikado* 1923

William J. Whillans as the Grand Inquisitor
– *The Gondoliers* 1928

Flo McKie as Mad Margaret
in *Ruddigore* 1929

The Gondoliers 1922
Robert Carlyle Wilson,
Belle Millar (later Mrs. Thomas Hamilton, Earlside),
Peggy Hunter, John Campbell (Marco, Gianetta, Tessa, Guiseppe).

The Gondoliers 1922
Flo McKie, Robert Wilson,
Mrs. James Tait (Duchess of Plaza Toro,
Duke of Plaza Toro, Casilda).

Iolanthe 1925
Greta Warwick (later Mrs. Joseph Baptie of Scaurend),
Belle Millar,
Robert Wilson (Fairy Queen, Iolanthe, Lord Chancellor).

Iolanthe 1925
Robert C. Wilson, Effie Thomson (later Mrs. John Campbell, grocer,
Liddesdale Road), Marie Johnston,
Robert Baxter (Earl Tolloller, Celia, Leila, Earl of Mountararat).

22

John Campbell   Robert Wilson
(Colonel Calverley)   (Reginald Bunthorne)
Patience 1921

Florence McKie
(Dame Carruthers)
The Yeomen of the Guard 1924

Tom Cowan Scott[17]
(Luiz)
The Gondoliers 1928

William J. Whillans   Greta Warwick
(Private Willis)   (Fairy Queen)
Iolanthe 1925

[17] Tom Cowan Scott (1898-1930) was a cousin of Elliot Cowan Smith (1891-1917), authority on the Hawick vernacular.

First produced by Sir George Dance with music by Edward Solomon in 1891 at the Savoy Theatre, London, it ran for an unremarkable 200 performances and certainly has nothing of the sparkle of Gilbert and Sullivan. Robert Wilson, to be sure, gave it a wide berth, but it was produced by the Society in the Town Hall for five nights commencing 19th March, 1926. It was described in the publicity as "Our Greatest Effort - - And in a New Direction!" In the event it turned out to be "Do Not Pass Go" and by May, 1926, the Society was committed to a restoration of its self respect in a performance of *The Pirates of Penzance*, scheduled for the end of that year. It was, in fact, to be Robert Wilson`s final performance with the Society, but not before setting up the Patrons` List with Treasurer William D. Turnbull in September, 1926.

Robert Wilson as Jack Point
The Yeomen Of The Guard 1924

The Patrons` List

Owing to the advent of the Entertainment Tax[18] in 1916, so much of a show`s financial residue was being taken by the Government that there was a danger that, in certain years of heavy production expenditure, there could be little or nothing left to distribute among charities. In 1926, however, the Act was amended, exempting charitable donation. The Society decided, therefore, to donate *all* surplus money following a show and create, as it were, a `sump fund`

---

[18]The tax was a massive source of revenue for the Government. Instituted in time of war, the rise of the cinema industry and its attendant profits made it almost impossible for any government to repeal. After decades of lobbying by film-makers, it was abolished in 1960 by the Macmillan administration.

The Nautch Girl 1926

BACK (l-r) - R.C. Wilson, Agnes Young, Robert Baxter, Doris Douglas, John Campbell
FRONT – Mary Taylor, Belle Millar

for incidental production costs, to be raised through the donations of patrons. In a letter with *pro forma* attached, circulated in the town and reproduced in the local Press, Wilson and Turnbull explained that –

> "…….in future, it will be impracticable to add anything to the Society's general fund against the possibility of a loss on any year's production, and while the Society does not anticipate any abatement in the generous public support extended to it during the past fifteen years, it feels that the members should be partially relieved of the responsibility for the heavy expenses in these productions. It has been suggested that many ladies and gentlemen in the town and district would willingly subscribe one guinea per annum to show their appreciation of the work done by the Society, and with this object in view, it is proposed to institute a List of Patrons in which the Society would like to include your name. For this yearly subscription mentioned there would be given two reserved tickets (complimentary) for the annual production………."[19]

Accordingly,1926 was a year of innovation for the Society and one of mixed results. The Patrons' List proved to be a success. Success in changing direction on the show front seemed less than convincing and a reversion to Gilbert and Sullivan with *The Gondoliers* in 1928 and *Ruddigore* in 1929 saw out the `twenties.

---

[19] The 1936 HAOS programme indicates 69 patrons; in 1939 the figure was 173; in 1956, 271; in 2010 there were 336, but it should be noted that the agreement on `complimentary` tickets has long since lapsed. Top price (reserved) tickets in 1926 were 4/9 so the Society received a donation from each patron of at least 11/6 which, in 2010, would be worth c. £20.

It had been a decade of transition. Bill Gaylor departed in 1924,[20] after a devastatingly slick performance as Shadbolt, the jailer in *The Yeomen Of The Guard*. Robert Wilson crowned his stage achievements as a highly polished Lord Chancellor in *Iolanthe* the following year, some twenty months before his own departure. By the end of the decade, the new men at the helm were John Campbell (1880-1950), President and Robert Baxter (1890-1956), Vice-President. Both had excellent `community` credentials, Campbell a top business manager and Baxter, a wool merchant operating from Stonefield Mills. Baxter was also an avid Common-Riding man, being Cornet Grieve`s Acting Father in 1929.

The vocal standards of this period were particularly high, to the extent that several members of the HAOS chorus, who would probably never wish for a more actively dramatic role, were highly capable `straight` soloists. Perhaps the most distinguished of them was tenor James Dalgleish who, using the pseudonym Allan Ramsay, went on to a professional singing career outwith Hawick besides making some noteworthy recordings of Hawick songs.[21]

The Pirates Of Penzance, December, 1926

Major General Stanley (Robert Wilson) with daughters
Back left – Isabel (Agnes Stewart); Back right – Kate (Dora Swanson);
Front left – Mabel (Agnes Young); Front right – Edith (Mary Taylor).

---

[20] It has been a matter of speculation that the allocation of the role of Lord Chancellor in *Iolanthe* for 1925 to Robert Wilson precipitated Gaylor`s departure. Gaylor had the role in 1914. Certainly, he never became a Patron nor did he take any part in the Golden Jubilee Celebration of 18th November, 1960 with other surviving founder members, although he did advertise his optician`s business in the Society`s programmes. He died 6/11/1963 at the age of 81.
[21] *Hawick* and *Hawick Cronies* were among those recorded for the old 78 rpm Beltona label. Dalgleish died at Galashiels 18/9/1959 aged 58. His brother, George Dalgleish, was the Hawick bootmaker.

Hawick Amateur Operatic Society

INSTITUTED 1910.

Affiliated with the National Operatic and Dramatic Association : : : :

LIST OF PATRONS

The Right Hon. The Earl of Minto
Katherine, Lady Usher, Wells
Sir Gilbert Eliott, Wolfelee
Sir Thomas Henderson, Langlands
Provost Fisher, 8 High Street
Thomas Aimers, Esq., Wilton Hill
Robert P. Appleby, Esq., 6 Bourtree Place
T. H. Armstrong, Esq., Ardenlea
Dr Barrie, Bridge Street
James Burnet, Esq., Langside
Robert Burns, Esq., Trinity Schoolhouse
Adam W. Barrie, Esq., Carrodyne
Thomas Brydon, Esq., 16 High Street
J. V. Bruce, Esq., British Linen Bank House
George Cairns, Esq., Sandbed
Robert Christie, Esq., Dunaird
Miss M. Drummond, High Street
Dr Davidson, Bridge Street
R. T. H. Doughty, Esq., Coille
George Davidson, Esq., Merlewood
T. R. Elliot, Esq., of Burnfoot
W. Scott Elliot, Esq., Greenbank
W. W. Flockhart, Esq., Ravenswood
Mrs M. H. C. Forman, Borthwickshiels.
Rev. W. Kenneth Grant, Cavers
Councillor T. N. Graham, Oliver Park
R. M. Hobkirk, Esq., 3 Allars Crescent
James Houston, Esq., Cragside
D. T. Hardie, Esq., Elmlea
Anthony Hunter, Esq., Twirlees Terrace
G. B. W. Hood, Esq., Rillmount
H. S. R. Innes, Esq., Westwood
Major W. A. Innes, The Firs
Lieut.-Col. J. Fyfe-Jamieson, Cavers
Mrs M. S. Laidlaw, Hazelwood
D. A. Marchbanks, Esq., 75 High Street

James Miller, Esq., 8 Douglas Road
D. McConnachie, Esq., Clairmont
J. E. D. Murray, Esq., Bridge Street Studio
R. Scott-Noble, Esq., Borthwickbrae
J. J. Oliver, Esq., Mayfield
John R. Purdom, Esq., Langheugh
John Park, Esq., Rosemount
W. Pennycook, Esq., 10 Beaconsfield Terr
Robert Pringle, Esq., Wood Norton
John Quin, Esq., Eastfield
W. S. Robson, Esq., East Stewart Place
John E. H. Scott, Esq., 37 High Street
J. R. Scoon, Esq., 19 Orchard Terrace
John Scoon, Esq., Gowanlea
Wm. Simpson, Esq., 8 Oliver Place
James B. Scott, Esq., Denholm Lodge
Mrs Janet Scott, Langlee
George Scott, Esq., Langlee
J. P. Scott, Esq., Parkside
James Scott, Esq., Heronhill
Dr Scott, Elm House
R. L. Scott, Esq., National Bank House
James Scoon, Esq., Duntroon
William Sharp, Esq., Rydal Bank
J. A. Robson-Scott, Esq., Newton, Jed
Bertram Talbot, Esq., Monteviot, Ancrum
John Turnbull, Esq., 18 N. Bridge Street
Walter Turnbull, Esq., 47 High Street
Miss Veitch, 2 Leaburn Drive
John J. Welch, Esq., Beaconsfield Terrace
George Wilson, Esq., Langhurst
W. E. Wilson, Esq., Riverview
I. Gray Wallis, Esq., Woodside
M. Williamson, Esq., Howlands
Colonel Younger, Hassendeanburn
Mrs Young, Thornlea

The following is a list of the productions given by the Society up to date :—

1911—H.M.S. Pinafore
1912—Pirates of Penzance
1913—The Mikado
1914—Iolanthe
1915-1919—No Productions
1920—H.M.S. Pinafore
1921—Patience
1922—The Gondoliers
1923—The Mikado
1924—Yeomen of the Guard

1925—Iolanthe
1926—The Nautch Girl
1927—Pirates of Penzance
1928—The Gondoliers
1929—Ruddigore
1930—A Country Girl
1931—The Arcadians
1932—The Damask Rose
1933—Florodora

Should any friends of the Society desire to have their names enrolled in the list of Patrons their subscriptions will be gratefully received by the Hon. Treasurer.

R. Deans & Co., Printers, 10 High Street, Hawick.

Patrons' List 1934 – predominantly the great and good of Hawick!

Chapter IV

THE INTER-WAR YEARS (2)

The `Thirties

1930 saw the Gilbert and Sullivan mould finally broken. There would be one `check` in 1934 with *The Mikado*, but a new dawn broke in 1930 with the Society's presentation of *A Country Girl* in the Pavilion Theatre. It was hardly a `modern` show even then, having first hit the London stage in 1902. A very British show, melodic certainly, but apart from Princess Mehelaneh's solo *Under the Deodar*, lacking the suavity and memorability of Lionel Monckton's later show *The Arcadians* (1909) with its *The Pipes Of Pan Are Calling, Arcady Is Ever Young* and *Charming Weather*. But *A Country Girl* was confirmation of the new direction the Society was taking and it would echo this burst of glory with *The Arcadians* the following year, 1931.

It is worth noting that HAOS `show week`(22nd-29th March, 1930) coincided with the coming of `the talkies` to Hawick cinema screens with the King's (Exchange) showing Victor McLaglen in *King of the Khyber Rifles*. To our own `stars`; the cast list of *The Arcadians* reads like a roll-call of pre-War Hawick `greats` – Robert Carlyle Wilson, William J. Whillans, John Johnstone, George B. Hall, Norman C. Henderson, Peggy Hunter, Andrew H. Wilkinson, Robert (Bert) Roddan, Florence McKie, Nainie Farries, Agnes Young, Margaret D. McKie, William Pickthall, William D. Turnbull and Walter Corbett. A brief shining star was Eileen Barrie.[22] Of her performance, the *Hawick Express* (26/3/1931) observed that "No-one received more clamant encores, and no-one more justly deserved recalls." Quite a testimonial in a cast which included the 1930 Borders Music Festival Gold Medallist (Robert Roddan) and Agnes Young, whom the *Scotsman*, no less, had lauded for a performance of Wallace's *Maritana* in Edinburgh's Empire Theatre.

A Country Girl 1930
Ella Beattie (later Mrs. A. Haig), ? ,
Margaret Cumming, Robert Roddan

---

[22] Mother of local solicitor Sandy Bannerman, she played only two shows with the Society – 1930, 1931.

The Arcadians also featured Flo McKie[23] and John Johnstone[24], who "were responsible for a great deal of merriment and applause." McKie and Johnstone were already established stage favourites. If Flo may be considered a doyenne of the Opera of the `twenties, it was a distinction which was excelled throughout the `thirties by Agnes Young who, in *The Arcadians*, took the part of Sombra, wowing the audience with her formidable vocal work – work of a standard which could only be challenged by that of Peggy Hunter as Chrysaea. For Flo McKie, however, although she lived to be ninety, this show was to be her last. She became Mrs. George Peacock in July, 1931 and, like so many before her (as seems to have been the accepted etiquette of the time) was henceforth lost to the Society.[25]

From the perspective of the twenty first century, it is challenging to imagine just what the reality of Hawick Opera was in the `thirties. There were no throat or face microphones; there was no amplification, full stop. To be in the Opera you had to be able to produce and project the natural voice. You had to be able to enunciate without enhancement. Variation of stage lighting was primitive; make-up was grease paint. The years in which shows were held in the Pavilion were blessed. The years, and there would be many, in which HAOS shows were presented in Hawick Town Hall, stretched the patience of the great loyal following of the Opera to the limit, in spite of the undoubtedly high standard of performance.

Despite all the frustrations of finding suitable accommodation for practice and performance, the `thirties were magical years for HAOS. The decade saw the musical scale new heights with the romantically charged music of Sigmund Romberg and Rudolf Friml dazzling the public through the cinematic and vocal artistry of stars like Jeanette Macdonald and Nelson Eddy and later, Webster Booth and his wife Anne Ziegler. With three cinemas, exposure to the glamour of the modern musical in Hawick was inevitable. The `pictures` formed a massive part of social entertainment, especially between 1930 and 1955. Queues in O`Connell Street for a blockbuster at the Pavilion were replicated at the King`s and the `Wee Thea` – a pattern of social discipline which extended nationwide.

In the Pavilion`s advertisement in the local Press for the week preceding HAOS`S presentation of *The Student Prince* in 1937, Jeanette Macdonald and Nelson Eddy were billed for *Rose Marie*, to be followed the next week by Irene Dunne and Paul Robeson in *Show Boat*. In March, 1931, the King`s (Exchange) had advertised *The Vagabond King* featuring Jeanette Macdonald in the week preceding HAOS`s presentation of *The Arcadians*. The Hawick public, then, was not uneducated with regard to the modern musical. It had something with which to compare its own talented sons and daughters, and it was not disappointed.

---

[23] Florence McKie was the elder daughter of John McKie, proprietor of the Glencairn Bar at the junction of Hawick`s O`Connell Street and High Street.

[24] Johnstone ran a butcher`s business at 6 Cross Wynd.

[25] The two other ladies would go the same way, Peggy Hunter becoming Mrs. Arthur Hinchecliffe in 1937 and moving to Wallsend and Agnes, Mrs. John Hunter in 1940 and moving to Selkirk. Peggy died at Annan in 1990 aged 88, Agnes at Peel, Galashiels in 1985 aged 80.

The Damask Rose 1932
An eighteen year-old John Huggan.
Later that year he set John Fairbairn`s *The Exile`s Dream* to music.
After the Second World War he became Head of Music at Galashiels Academy and
was briefly Musical Director of Galashiels Amateur Operatic Society.

Group from *The Arcadians* 1931

Only six can be positively identified. BACK – Mary Murray,   ?   , Agnes Stewart, Nainie Farries,   ?   ,
FRONT – (from left) – Jean Pringle, Christina Murdoch, Jenny Townsend. Mary Murray was the mother of
George and Sybil Storie, prominent members after the Second World War.
Her grandchildren – Roger, Vanessa and Alan Storie were in the Opera in the `70s and `80s.

These people could dance, sing and act and be heard and enjoyed without the assistance of microphones or other technical aids.

Private music and elocution lessons were much in demand. At the end of August, 1936, nine private music teachers advertised on the front page of *Hawick News* – Messrs. Hessey, William Lightheart, George Smith, Frank Simpson, David B. Simpson, Misses. Agnes Young, G.R. Brockie, Agnes Miller and Mrs. T. Angus. There were others such as Mrs. Walter Turnbull, wife of one of HAOS`s founder members. Hawick was a highly musically literate town. But importantly, and complementary to this, was the large number of dramatic societies in churches and mills and other organisations such as the PSA Brotherhood.

The Arcadians of 1931 really boosted the confidence of the Society in staging musicals. As a theatre piece it had enjoyed the third longest run of any show up to its opening at London`s Shaftesbury Theatre in 1909 and, for the amateur society of the `thirties, it was only really surpassed by the suave, cosmopolitan shows with music by Sigmund Romberg and Rudolf Friml, notably *The Desert Song*, *The Student Prince* and *The New Moon* by the former and *Rose Marie* and *The Vagabond King* by the latter. All, with the exception of *The New Moon*, were staged by Hawick Amateur Operatic Society in the politically turbulent five years before the outbreak of the Second World War.

The presentation of *The Desert Song* in 1935 was a landmark in the Society`s development. It was, for its time, the Opera`s first big universally acclaimed `modern` show and such was its popularity that, for the first time, a "Special Matinee" was offered on Saturday, 23rd March, 1935. This was, in the opinion of several members of the Society, a perilous move, concern being expressed that the Saturday evening performance might be adversely affected owing to cast exhaustion. But the Saturday matinee performance has remained ever since, with the exception of 1966 when, owing to refurbishment, the Town Hall could not be effectively `blacked out`. It became apparent, from an economic point of view, that the matinee, as a source of increased revenue, was indispensable. For not unrelated reasons, the word *voluntary* was to disappear from the Society`s printed programmes after 1939. Henceforth, a fixed price programme would be the form.

The cast-listed principals for *The Desert Song* are iconic in the annals of HAOS; Andrew H. Wilkinson, John Johnstone, William Whillans, David Stothart, Robert Roddan, Madge Gladstone, Sidney Irvine, Ian Carruthers, Agnes Young, Robert Baxter, Adam Hogg, Maimie B. Clark, Margaret D. McKie, John Forrest, Peggy Hunter, Betty Wilson and Hamilton B. Little. The chorus, to boot, was studded with competent and proven soloists like Nainie Farries, Ina Wintrope,[26] Walter Corbett, Walter Elder, Elliot Kyle, Tom Shearman and Archie Romanis. It also included three founder members – Misses. Sarah Armstrong, Jean Gladstone and Agnes Stewart (all former minor principals).

---

[26] Ina Wintrope gave the first public performance of Albert V. Budge`s song *My Borderland* in 1952.

Regarding principal roles, Agnes Young`s and Peggy Hunter`s stars had been in the ascendant since the mid-`twenties, but they had been joined towards the end of that decade by those of Margaret D. McKie (younger sister of Flo) and Maimie B. Clark (a teacher in the primary department of Hawick High School). David Stothart, the local saddler and sports shop owner, had had a fairly low profile in Gilbert and Sullivan days, but with the shift to musicals, he seemed to blossom, becoming the unrivalled master of comedy. Stothart was the kind of natural comic that all operatic societies cherish; he could elicit laughter simply by walking on stage. He was also a gifted reciter. One of his co-humorists of later years, Betty Howarth (a niece of Jean Gladstone), recalled him as having almost a `rubber face`, such was his talent for quizzical expression. In *The Desert Song*, his co-humorist was Maimie B. Clark. The *Hawick Express* (21/3/1935) ventured the opinion that "One could scarcely imagine these roles (Benjamin Kidd and Susan) to be more aptly cast."

Madge Gladstone as Azuri
The Desert Song 1935

Adam Hogg`s[27] performance as Red Shadow was the pinnacle of his amateur stage career. An employee of Innes, Henderson & Co and a newcomer in that season, he had been greatly involved, together with Stothart, as a producer in the drama side of the PSA movement. *The Hawick Express* noted that he "earned unstinted applause for his soldierly bearing and commanding presence in a splendid deliveration of a character so romantic and appealing ..." He went on to play other leading roles in the years up to the War, but his stage reputation was defined by this part. Andrew H. Wilkinson[28] was really Robert Carlyle Wilson`s natural successor as Hawick`s number one tenor and he was to prove to be Agnes Young`s ideal stage partner. His doubling, as Sid El Car, with Hogg in *One Alone*, was devastating. Agnes`s ability should not be underestimated. She was Usher Hall standard and in demand as a guest artiste in the Capital.

The Desert Song validated a more earnest approach to the place of dance in musical theatre. In the Hawick production, Madge (Margaret) Gladstone, youngest of the three Gladstone girls involved with HAOS (daughters of Walter Gladstone, knitwear manufacturer), captivated the Pavilion audiences with her portrayal of Azuri. Since 1930, the Society had employed a designated dance mistress, among the more notable being Miss. Margot Tullis of Kirkcaldy.

---

[27] Adam Hogg was an uncle of Mrs. Margaret Logan (Robertson), former playing member, now on the Opera`s Social Committee.
[28] Wilkinson was the great grandfather of the Cornet of 2003, Greg McLeod.

Lady Principals of the 'Thirties

Maimie B. Clark
(Gretchen)
The Student Prince 1937

Peggy Hunter
(Clementina)
The Desert Song 1935

Agnes Young
(Katherine de Vaucelles)
The Vagabond King 1939

Margaret D. McKie
(Lady Jane)
Rose Marie 1936

The run-around `ditty` dances which had found acceptance in Gilbert and Sullivan would no longer suffice for the modern musical. For *The Desert Song*, Miss. Brunton of Edinburgh was engaged and, apart from the years when Miss. Frances Davis of London, was producer, a dance mistress or choreographer was *de rigueur*. Another reason, of course, for the elevation of dance was the pervasive influence of the cinema with artistes like Fred Astaire (for example in *Top Hat,* 1935) and the dazzling kaleidoscopic routines of that most innovative of choreographers, Busby Berkeley. By the end of the twentieth century, HAOS would be presenting dance routines undreamt of and unimaginable in its Gilbert and Sullivan days.

The Desert Song, besides being the last for which J.E.D. Murray did make-up, confirmed the end of the long association with the first producer, John Brewster. He had taken a year out in the 1932-33 season when Mr. Gordon Stamford, London produced *Florodora*, but returned for his last season, 1933-34, to produce his third *Mikado* for Hawick. *The Desert Song* was

David O. Stothart
in characteristic pose as Benjamin Kidd
The Desert Song 1935

subsequently entrusted to another Edinburgh man, Mr. Jack Lennox.This show was also a first for Miss. Eleanor Beveridge (1897-1971) as Society Pianist following the death in 1934 of Eustace Davidson at only thirty eight years of age. She had been a member of the Society since 1932, taking a minor principal role in *Florodora*, but it is as pianist for over thirty years, latterly as Mrs. Dalgleish, that she is best remembered; yet another example of the dedicated key members who hold a society together.

The Society`s Silver Jubilee

Such had been the success of *The Desert Song* that there was genuine concern that the choice of show for 1936 – the Silver Jubilee performance – might result in anti-climax. So great had been the public demand for the 1935 show that the first day booking queue had, at one point, extended from Grant`s Music Warehouse (next to the former Post Office) to the SMT garage in Dovemount Street. The show`s balance sheet had shown £277[29] available for charitable disbursement after meeting all production expenses. Could this be sustained, let alone bettered? The Society`s AGM on 23rd April, 1935 recorded that "no decision was come to with regard to next year`s production." There was much to mull over but, in due course, the resumption of practices in Johnstone`s Central Rooms[30] was announced for Monday, 7th

---

[29] Around £15,000 in equivalent value today.
[30] Johnstone`s Central Rooms in O` Connell Street are today occupied by the Fitness Centre.

Silver Jubilee Celebrations 1935 – Full Company

BACK – Ina Wintrope, W. Elder, Gladys Wood, S. Irvine, May Watters, D.C. Scott, Maimie Aitken, J. Johnstone, Agnes Young, W. Robson, Elizabeth McKennie, M.C. Patterson, Mrs. A.B. Hogg, J. Kennedy, Jean Pringle, R. Roddan, Susie Thomson, T.A. Shearman, Marie Lamb, J. Stewart, Mrs. Huggan.

MIDDLE – Jessie Hepburn, J. Forrest, Agnes Scoon, A.H. Wilkinson, Maimie Clark, G. Aitken, Nancy Aitken, H. Storrie, May Barrie, E.O. Kyle, Eleanor Beveridge (Pianist), D.O. Stothart, Mary Wallace, A.Oliver, Mrs. A.B. Haig, W.J. Whillans, Margaret D. McKie, A. Hogg, Betty Wilson, Walter Turnbull, Isa Fairbairn.

FRONT - Nainie Farries, H.B. Little (Hon. Secretary), Annie Miller, T.E. Shortreed (Hon. Treasurer), Jenny Townsend, Wm. Campbell (Hon. Conductor), Agnes Stewart, Robert Wilson (Hon. President), Jean Gladstone, John Campbell (President), Mrs. H. McCallum, Robert Baxter (Vice-President), Sarah Armstrong, William D. Turnbull, Barbara Scott, Walter Corbett, Madge McCartney.

Unable to be present were Madge Gladstone, Mrs. Whitelaw, N.C. Henderson, I. Carruthers, and J. Duncan.

October, 1935 at 8 p.m. and the show was *Rose Marie*, with music by Rudolf Friml. The producer was to be Gordon Stamford, London, who had already produced for the Society in 1933.

Rose Marie ticked all the boxes for potential excellence and financial success. It was in the same league as *The Desert Song*, with unforgettable melodies that had been broadcast on radio and sold on gramophone records and sheet music. Jeanette Macdonald and Nelson Eddy had imprinted it in the psyche of most `picture goers`. The Society`s confidence was at an all-time high and they had at their disposal a purpose built theatre with all the desirable requisites for performers and the comfort of the audience. At the time of its choice, however, what the Society did not know was that *Rose Marie* would be its final show in the Pavilion.

Rose Marie opened on Tuesday, 17th March, 1936 in the Pavilion Theatre for a five night run plus matinee to unalloyed public delight. There was an upbeat mood in the nation at large with the Accession of Edward VIII at the end of January that year and *Rose Marie* came sufficiently early in the calendar to avoid the gloom of the Abdication in early December. The costumes for *Rose Marie* were spectacular, especially those of the Totem Girls. The whole show radiated a festive atmosphere, entirely in keeping with the celebratory sentiments of the Society`s Silver Jubilee. The ever popular Musical Director, Willie Campbell, received great cheers as he occupied the podium. His brother John, the Society`s President, returned to the stage after a break of two years, to give his final costumed performance, as Sergeant Malone, singing "with fitting breadth and richness."

Sports Dance – *Rose Marie* 1936

May Barrie, May Watters, ?, Nainie Farries, Louie Huggan, Susie Thomson, Jean Pringle, ?, Isa Waters

Andrew Wilkinson went from strength to strength as Jim Kenyon, Agnes Young "being altogether excellent" in the title role. The *Hawick Express* (26/3/1936), continuing, described "a very winsome and appealing Rose Marie......popular opinion would concede that she was the star vocalist of the company......full of interest, while her singing, as usual, was brilliant and fascinating to a degree." The songs *Rose Marie* and *Indian Love Call* were, of course, already known universally as showstoppers.

David Orkney Stothart`s natural gift for humour was exploited fully and enhanced by "an exceptional talent for dancing and light singing." He was, as Hard Boiled Herman, partnered by Margaret McKie who made "a lovely and vivacious Lady Jane." Their attractive duet, *Why Shouldn`t We* was described in the same newspaper as "one of the choicest titbits of the play, accompanied as it was by some remarkably clever dancing."

Rose Marie is a sumptuous schmaltzy piece of music theatre, the male chorus a sturdy company of `Mounties` and, of course, the special troupe of Totem Girls, adding to the spectacle. The show actively involved six founder members; Misses. Sarah Armstrong, Jean Gladstone and Agnes Stewart, along with Messrs. John Campbell, William Campbell and Walter Turnbull[31] in his first participation since 1923. The production, according to the local Press, "may be said to have filled the very highest expectations – with the possible exception of *The Desert Song* which marked a new departure for the Society........Nothing finer than *Rose Marie* has been produced locally for a very long time." It is certainly noteworthy that, for the `thirties, in the eyes of the *cognoscenti*, the yardstick against which all productions were to be measured was *The Desert Song*.

By 1936, it really seemed as if HAOS was on a roll. It seemed to have everything; outstanding soloists, deft, versatile comedians/comediennes, increasing awareness of the contribution of dance and a chorus from which could be drawn at least another half dozen soloists, among them May Barrie, Mary Boles, Wat Elder, Norman Henderson[32] and Harry Storrie.[33] For *The Student Prince* of 1937, the Society engaged Miss. Frances Davis, London as producer – a piece of real good fortune. There was only one seemingly intractable problem – Hawick Town Hall.

In the Autumn of 1936, the Pavilion Theatre underwent internal reconstruction which rendered future stage productions impossible. The members of HAOS were horrified to discover that, although there was no problem in hiring the Town Hall after almost a decade at the Pavilion, nothing had changed in their absence. If anything, things had deteriorated.

---

[31] Fruiterer and confectioner at 47 High Street, his wife Julia (née Needham) ATCL a singing teacher. He was organist of the Congregational Church for twenty years and of Wilton Church until his death in 1943. He had the part of Earl Tolloller in *Iolanthe* (1914).

[32] Norman Henderson was the son of William Henderson, 14 High Street, bookseller and Opera booking agent after the closure of Adam Grant`s at the beginning of 1938.

[33] Harry Storrie became Hawick`s Official Common-Riding Song Singer after the War.

At the Town Council's meeting on 15th May, 1937, improvements to the Town Hall in the light of a public statement issued by the Society[34] were discussed. Provost Fisher said that he was "more than ever convinced of the difficulties under which the Opera Society were working." By the beginning of November that year he had changed his mind. The advice the Council had been given for remedial action showed that such would be "too costly." They would, instead, be looking for a "generous donor."

Rose Marie 1936

D. O. Stothart (Herman), Margaret McKie (Lady Jane), Adam Hogg (Emile).

But there would be none. The local Press headlines of 10th November, 1937 proclaimed, "Town Hall Projects Definitely Dropped – No New Hall – No Alterations." The disenchantment rumbled on. In April, 1939, William S. Robson, Secretary and Treasurer of Hawick Choral Society bemoaned the situation at their AGM, claiming –

"... the Society's principal handicap lies in the non-existence of a suitable hall in the town for public entertainment. When this defect will be remedied I cannot predict, but so far as I can judge from the present political situation, we are dependent for this improvement rather less on the wisdom of a Town Council or the generosity of a public benefactor, than on the chance, or mischance, of a well-placed bomb."

Staging a production in the Town Hall would continue to tax the ingenuity of producers and try the patience of audiences. No producer demonstrated that ingenuity more convincingly than Frances Davis, producer of the three shows before the War – *The Student Prince* (1937), *Viktoria And Her Hussar* (1938) and *The Vagabond King* (1939). Miss. Davis, who had been coaching amateur societies for some five years at the time of her engagement by HAOS was, herself, a stage professional, steeped in song and dance as well as drama. She was the Society's most comprehensive producer – she did everything, including the choreography, and anything that came within her remit was executed with succinct professionalism. (She did several years with the Society after the War, and those who recall her do so with a mixture of awe and admiration).

---

[34] This 'open letter' signed on behalf of HAOS by John Campbell, President, Robert Baxter, Vice-President and Hamilton B. Little, General Secretary appeared in the local Press in March, 1937. Though couched in diplomatic terms (not *blaming* the Town Council) it nevertheless laid the whole issue bare for comment and public discussion.

Press release image of Frances Davis 1937

The Student Prince 1937
Tom Shearman (Toni) and Andrew H. Wilkinson (Prince Kart Franz)

The Student Prince 1937
Robert Roddan, Adam Hogg, Hamilton B. Little.

Allan Beattie, in his `Musical and Dramatic Notes` in the *Hawick Express* (18/12/37) reveals –

> "Miss. Davis takes great pains in her arrangement of the various scenes down to the smallest detail, and if the company have to work hard now, they have the satisfaction of knowing that they are working up to a successful climax which can only come through perseverance and hard practice."

Some fifteen months later, the same newspaper (29/3/39) noted that she –

> "..never earned greater credit than by this excellent production (*The Vagabond King)* in the limitations of the Town Hall stage. Those who have seen her work at rehearsals will marvel the more that one small figure can hold all the energy, persistence and skill she has shown in striving for perfection."

Miss. Davis would arrive in Hawick a week or two before Christmas to put the show `on the floor`. She might remain a week or ten days depending on progress. Usually, she lodged with the Stothart family. She would return about a fortnight before the dress rehearsal when members of the company would be expected to be available every night if required.

Of the prestigious inter-War shows, Sigmund Romberg`s *The Student Prince* was, arguably, the most romantic and most melodically appealing, the story one of young love frustrated

The Student Prince 1937
D.O. Stothart (Luiz), John Johnstone (Dr. Engels), A.H. Wilkinson (Prince),
John Forrest (Innkeeper), Agnes Young (Kathie), Maimie B. Clark (Gretchen).

by the barriers of rank and duty. The songs were truly memorable – *Golden Days*, *Drinking Song*, *Overhead the Moon is Beaming*, *Just We Two*, and *Deep In My Heart, Dear*. The Teutonic setting and, by 1937, the seeming inevitability of war with Nazi Germany, brought to the performance a certain poignancy. Was this all going to go and did things really have to be this way?

Hawick`s production of 1937 did not disappoint. The principals were again Agnes Young, Andrew H. Wilkinson, David Stothart, Maimie Clark and Margaret McKie. Andrew Wilkinson`s boyish good looks and fine tenor voice made him an outstanding Prince Karl Franz and the comedy was sustained with panache by David Stothart. Little more can be said of Agnes Young; her position as doyenne of the Opera in the `thirties was unassailable. It is the opinion of those who remember her performances that, vocally, she remains unsurpassed in the annals of the Society. The *Hawick Express (30/3/1938)* noted –

> " .. lucky is the Society to have so grand a singer to take the role of which good singing is the essence (*Viktoria*). Miss. Young may sometimes find the more dramatic situations a little difficult, but her acting is splendid, nevertheless and even if it were not, her singing would make the choice for the part inevitable."

As with every operatic society, there develops from time to time a core (and corps) of key performers, so it was in HAOS at this point – Agnes Young, Andrew Wilkinson, Margaret McKie, Maimie Clark, David Stothart, John Johnstone, Adam Hogg, Nainie Farries and Sidney Irvine. By the late `thirties they had been joined by John Forrest and David Hobbs. Wilkinson`s rise in public approbation continued unabated through 1938 (*Viktoria And Her Hussar*) and he crowned his achievements in 1939 as Francois Villon, *The Vagabond King*. Having joined the Society in 1929, it is fair to say that this was indeed his decade. David Stothart`s work elicited the comment in 1938 that he was "the star comedian, and everything he touches turns to mirth." Significant newcomers to HAOS just before the War were Archie Romanis, of the personnel welfare staff of Innes, Henderson & Co., Adam R. Hogg, David

Viktoria And Her Hussar 1938
Maimie Clark (Riquette), A.H. Wilkinson (Kolta), Agnes Young (Viktoria),
Adam Hogg (Porkelty), Syd Irvine (Hegedu), Mary Boles (O Lia San).

Hobbs, Roland (Ronnie) Stormont,[35] Harry Storrie and Tom Crawford.

By 1939, war was inevitable; the signs were all around; gas masks, air raid shelters, blackout enforcement and a thirst for escapism that had never been so strong. Never had the booking (at Henderson`s, Bookseller, that year) been so prompt or so heavy. There was even a threat to the dress rehearsal for *The Vagabond King* on 27th March owing to ARP (Air Raid Precautions) drill scheduled for that evening. In the event, it was announced that " Hawick was to be a place of complete darkness for the two hours from ten o` clock to midnight." The dress rehearsal proceeded without incident albeit at an earlier hour. The assumption that life would continue normally (although no-one believed it) was the only positive way forward, so HAOS made its choice of show for 1940, the Town Hall being reserved for the last week in February for *The Belle of New York*. It was an old show, dating from 1897 but, in the event, it didn`t matter. The declaration of war on Sunday, 3rd September, 1939 swept away all plans and dreams. The Society had been here before.

Viktoria And Her Hussar 1938
Cissie (Jessie) Aitken, dancer.

The Vagabond King 1939
D.O. Stothart (Tabarie), Margaret McCartney (Lady Mary), Tom P. Crawford (Le Dain).

---

[35] Ronnie Stormont`s grandchildren, David and Lesley Stormont, took the childrens` parts in *South Pacific* (1985). Lesley (Mrs. Fraser) is now a prominent member of HAOS as is her sister Leanne Turnbull and their cousin (also Ronnie`s granddaughter), Gillian Patterson.

Chapter V

THE FORTUNES OF WAR

A pattern, similar to that which had occurred during the First World War, affecting HAOS, developed. The show projected for 1940 was, of course, abandoned and there were one or two instances of HAOS members performing for the war effort. Betty Wilson, Nainie Farries, James Combe and Adam Hogg, accompanied on the piano by local accountant and First World War veteran John J. Welch,[36] gave a concert for the British Legion at Stobs on 26th September, 1940, but most of the younger men of the Society were duly required for military service. Women were also taken. Nancy Aitken went to the RAF as did her brother, George, he being awarded the DFM in 1944.

The increased emotional intensity of wartime life brought a spate of marriages and consequent departures to other areas of the country – Agnes Young to Selkirk as Mrs. John Hunter, Margaret McKie to Edinburgh as Mrs. Bruce Smith and Nainie Farries eventually to London as Mrs. Walter Lear. Two Aitken sisters – Mary (Maimie) and Jessie (Cissie) married two Manson brothers from Glasgow. To HAOS, these happy occasions represented loss. But no loss was greater felt in the Operatic fraternity than that occasioned by the death of Sergeant Observer Adam Hogg, RAF (Red Shadow of 1935), killed in Britain while on a training programme in July, 1941.

A further domestic contingency resulting from the War was the creation of a `British Restaurant` in Hawick Town Hall with the consequent emplacement of cooking equipment and boilers on a large area of the stage – a development with serious implications for the resuscitation of the Society after the War.

The exigencies of war, however, resulted in an upsurge of smaller scale entertainments in churches, church halls and in the Library Hall. The frontal area of the Town Hall stage could still be used, but anything requiring depth was out of the question. The Junior Drama Group flourished to the advantage of stage-hungry youngsters like Jean Whillans and Shiela Laing, who were equally at ease on the concert platform. In the latter capacity, they were joined by Jean Turnbull – a small girl with a very large voice.

As normalisation proceeded following victory in 1945, Hawick Drama Club presented Shaw`s *Arms And The Man* in 1946 with David Hobbs in the leading role. Newly `demobbed` Archie Romanis also took part. A year later, it was J.M. Barrie`s *What Every Woman Knows,* featuring David Hobbs and Maimie Clark. The Drama Club`s 1948 production, Emlyn Williams` *The Light Of Heart* confirmed Jean Whillans in a leading role alongside David Hobbs, Maimie

---

[36] John J. Welch, C.A. was a music enthusiast. He played the oboe in the HAOS orchestra, December, 1926 – *The Pirates of Penzance*, 1932 – *The Damask Rose*, 1933 – *Florodora*, but he was really a Choral Society man.

Clark and Leyden Martin (daughter of HAOS`s Honorary President, Robert Wilson). The point, of course, is cross-fertilisation of societies. Most of these people were `Opera` people or up-and- coming Opera people. HAOS was among the last clubs and societies to restart after the Second World War. The problem was an old one – the Town Hall. After much discussion, argument, and opposition from trades unions, the Town Council, at its meeting on 3rd February, 1947, took the decision to close the British Restaurant.

Chapter VI

THE OPERA IN THE BRAVE NEW WORLD

From The Top

Following the Council`s decision, HAOS`s office bearers moved quickly and a meeting was announced for Friday, 21st February, 1947, in the Library Hall. Over seventy attended. Later, thirty nine opera enthusiasts, some as young as fifteen, put forward their names as prospective members. John Campbell, President, was in the chair. William Whillans, Secretary, was asked to open negotiations for the production of a Gilbert and Sullivan opera, to ascertain costs, etcetera and to investigate the possibility of re-engaging Frances Davis as Producer.

A further meeting was called for Monday, 7th April, 1947 in St. John`s Masonic Hall. In a change of heart, it was decided that the show to open the new era would be Monckton`s *A Country Girl*. Old habits die hard, but the Society was sticking with the musical. Production was scheduled for the end of February, 1948. The strength of the resuscitated Society was over sixty, with 28 new members having enrolled in the course of six weeks.

A tremendous burden fell on Secretary Whillans. Although Campbell and Baxter were President and Vice-President respectively, Whillans was effectively the Society`s chief executive officer; everything, at some point, passed through him. He may, in fact, be considered the architect of the Society`s post-War revival. His indispensable colleague was Tom Shortreed (1887-1968), the Hon. Treasurer, a clerk in the hosiery trade. Their stage musical association stretched back to the chorus of *HMS Pinafore* (1920). The Society was in safe hands. Practices for *A Country Girl* began in St. John`s Masonic Hall on 1st September 1947. Willie

Willie Campbell,
founder member, and M.D. (1919-1950)
with Eleanor Dalgleish (pianist) 1950

Campbell, who had resigned as Musical Director, was persuaded to return to help the revival. With the unavailability of Frances Davis, Mr. J. Hebden Foster, Edinburgh, was engaged as Producer. Madame Beatrice Miranda,[37] also of Edinburgh, was appointed to assist him in production, but with a special remit as dancing instructress.

A Country Girl opened in the Town Hall for a six-night run plus matinee on 23rd February, 1948, curtain up 8 p.m. Prices ranged from 2/- (10p) to 6/- (30p).[38] Noteworthy was the arrival of four talented girl principals – Maimie Beattie, Shiela Laing, Jean Turnbull and Jean Whillans taking the roles, respectively, of Madame Sophie, Marjorie, Princess Mehelaneh and Nan. For Jean Whillans, daughter of the Society`s indefatigable Secretary, it was the beginning of an active relationship with the Society which was to last for over sixty years as performer and producer. Jean Turnbull, who had, according to the local Press, sung *Under the Deodar* "outstandingly well",was destined to be Rio Rita in the following year`s production, joining the chorus of *The New Moon* in 1950 in which year she married William Hart[39] of the male chorus and was henceforth lost to the Opera. No such notion impeded Jean Whillans, who continued with increasing dedication following her marriage to Neil Wintrope in 1951. Shiela Laing became a much acclaimed principal over the following decade until she became Mrs. John Paul in 1960 and moved to Glasgow. Likewise, Maimie Beattie married Ernest Rafferty of Blackpool in 1948 and left the town.

Jean Turnbull – Princess Mehelaneh
A Country Girl 1948

Walter S. Smith was the most notable new male principal of 1948, taking the role of Geoffrey Challinor. The remaining principals in *A Country Girl* were well-respected pre-War figures – Archie Romanis, David Stothart, David Hobbs, John Forrest, Wat Elder, Elliot Kyle, Ian Carruthers, John Johnstone, Syd Irvine, Maimie B. Clark and Betty Wilson. But there were other new names in the chorus and among the attendants, names which would come into clearer focus in future shows – Bill Robson, Ian MacDonald, David Thomson and Betty Howarth. Betty recently recalled that, as a child, all she wanted was to be in the Opera. Her parents had been founder members; her brother George had got in in 1937. Betty, however, failed her audition, but was taken on as an `Indian Attendant` to the Rajah of Bhong in *A Country Girl.* Her perseverance paid off and, after making the chorus of *Rio Rita* (1949)*,* she landed the part of Julie, the maid in *The New Moon* (1950), before establishing herself as the talented comedienne of the company as Phoebe, the English maid in *The Quaker*

---

[37] Her previous tenuous connection with HAOS was that she was mentor and teacher of pre-War Opera favourite Agnes Young.
[38] Prices for 2010 were £6 and £10.
[39] For many years Jean and Billy Hart owned and ran the shop on the corner of Princes Street and Havelock Street.

Girl (1951) when she partnered Archie Romanis. The *Hawick Express* (21/2/51) reported – "What good fun these two were and how admirably they played their parts in both song and clowning."

It is interesting to reflect on how many occasions in show business human tragedy can conspire to threaten all aspirations for a performance. The Hawick Society has had its share of such situations. *A Country Girl* was so affected twelve days before its opening when William Anderson, a local upholsterer, who was to be playing The Rajah of Bhong, died suddenly. In true `show must go on` tradition, Archie Romanis stepped into the breach and John Johnstone from the chorus took Archie`s part as Granfer Mummery.

Perhaps the most enduring icon of the post-War period was Jean Whillans (later Wintrope). Her sheer dedication and professionalism set her in the top rank of HAOS`s pantheon. She became, in the `fifties and `sixties, what Agnes Young had been in the `thirties, her performances irreproachable. Of the nineteen shows in which she appeared, she led in seventeen, the title role in *Rio Rita* (1949) going to Jean Turnbull (Mrs. Hart) and the leading female role in *Show Boat* (1972) – Magnolia – going to Myra McLeod.

Archie Romanis – the Rajah of Bhong
A Country Girl 1948

Dancers in *Rio Rita* 1949

LEFT TO RIGHT - Margaret Ferguson, Shiela Laing, Betty Howarth, Nancy Aitken, Betty Clarke, Charlotte Millar, Margaret Mable. FRONT – Audrey Lyon. Margaret Mable was the mother of Pat Lyle, leading lady of *Flower Drum Song* 1982 and Audrey Lyon mother of Shelagh Duncan (Secretary 2002-2010).

The Desert Song 1952
Paula Ritchie (Azuri)
and Ian Carruthers (Captain Paul Fontaine)

Nina Rosa 1953
Jean Wintrope (Nina) and Bill Tait (Haines)

Bill Whillans, Secretary of HAOS, receives his NODA long service medal from his daughter, Jean Wintrope following *Nina Rosa* 1953.
Also pictured are (l-r) D.O. Stothart, John Forrest, Tom Shortreed, Frances Davis and the NODA representative.

Many will have their own special memory of Jean Wintrope`s never-less-than-class acts Would it be as Anna Glavari in *The Merry Widow* (1965), Anna Leonowens in *The King And I* (1964), Eliza Doolittle in *My Fair Lady* (1969) or Rosalinda in *Pink Champagne* (1954) or Jean in one of the remaining thirteen or, indeed, all? The *Hawick Express* (25/2/48) observed that " there is a confidence, a `polished` finish and a natural verve about her work which marks her out for many leading roles to come." Prophetic words. Jean`s final costumed appearance with HAOS was as Julie in *Show Boat* (1972), but she was far from finished with the Society, returning in the Autumn of 1977 to produce the next two shows – *Bless The Bride* (1978) and *The King And I* (1979).

The Desert Song 1952
The inimitable David Hobbs (Benjamin) with Betty Howarth (Susan).

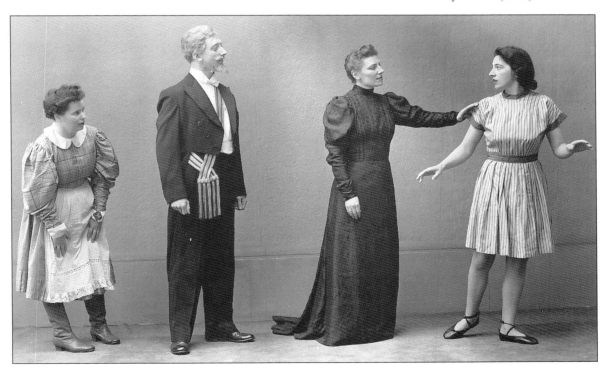

Balalaika 1956
Betty Howarth (Masha), Ian Rorrison (Prince Karajin), Shiela Laing (Mme. Petrova) and Jean Wintrope (Lydia Marakov).

Hungarian Dancers – *Pink Champagne* 1954
BACK – Pat Stormont, Kitty Douglas, Margaret Knox, Nancy Aitken, Cathie Hay
FRONT – Olga Mowatt, Maimie Richardson, June Law.

Other lady members of the Society made their marks with sterling performances in this period, which it is convenient to review up to 1986 – the post-War years (the Austerity) and the `third quarter`. Maimie B. Clark and Betty Wilson were still well to the fore in the late `forties and early `fifties. Shiela Laing was probably the most prominent supporting principal among the new intake of 1947-48. Among her memorable roles were Sally McBride in *Love From Judy* (1957), Adele in *Pink Champagne* (1954) and Ado Annie in *Oklahoma* (1955). Her final appearance with HAOS as the eponymous heroine of *Annie, Get Your Gun* (1959) was marked by controversy because a `smart Alec` reviewer for the *Hawick Express* (11/3/59) decided to show off his dubious knowledge and take a pot shot at the Society, tearing the whole production to shreds. Of the show itself he wrote –

> "*Annie Get Your Gun* follows the cult of the primitive and is crude in both theatre and the other arts which found favour in America after the War, and have since spread to Europe."

He then proceeded to slate the producer and entire cast. The reaction in the town was vitriolic, so much so that in the following week`s edition of the newspaper, the editor was obliged to admit that, of several letters received on the subject, only one could be printed, such was the vituperative nature of the remainder. The letter published, from a Mr. Wood of Galashiels, observed –

> "...the Hawick Society should congratulate themselves on having a member like Shiela Laing. Many other societies would be happy to have her services."

Ladies` Chorus – *Annie, Get Your Gun* 1959
BACK – (l-r) Betty Burnet, Linda Turnbull, Betty Tierney, Rita Taylor, Christine Lyon, Gwen Lowes, Betty Howarth, Rena Towsend, Maisie Ormiston.
MIDDLE – May Matthews, Maureen Black, Margaret Sullivan, Margaret Robertson, Irene Cowen, Eileen Scott.
FRONT – Morag Smith, Nancy Aitken, Ada Robson.

It was true, and she is still remembered with affection in Hawick. The incident is a reminder that the local Press has not always been as benign towards the Society as it has been of recent years. Adverse Press comment, it will be recalled, may have played a part in the demise of the original Hawick Amateur Opera Company (HAOC) back in 1899. On the other hand, balanced, informed comment helps posterity to judge `standard`.

Oklahoma rehearsal 1953 – Dream Ballet sequence
BACK – (l-r) Cathie Hay, Kitty Douglas, Nancy Aitken, Evelyn Kersel – Olga Mowatt on shoulders of Tom Hibbert.
MIDDLE – Gilbert Cowper, Jack Douglas, Jack Stewart.   FRONT - ? , Charlie Milligan.

Other memorable female performances over this period would have to include those of Cathie Little as Laurey in *Oklahoma* (1955), Vera Mundell (Pringle) as *Rose Marie* (1960), Jean Rorrison (Watson) as Lady Thiang in *The King And I* (1964),Rita Storie as Ado Annie in *Oklahoma* (1967) and as Miss. Adelaide in *Guys And Dolls* (1986), Maisie Hill as Laurey in *Oklahoma* (1967), Sally Robson as the Mother Abbess in *The Sound of Music* (1971), Alison Seeley as Queenie in *Show Boat* (1972) Brenda Walker (Whyte) as Julie Jordan in *Carousel* (1973), Letta Dalgleish as Nellie Forbush in *South Pacific* (1975, 1985) and her sister, Myra Mcleod as Margot Bonvalet in *The Desert Song* (1976), Christine Lyon as the redoubtable Mrs. Sally Adams in *Call Me Madam* (1977), sharing the role with Rita Storie, Patricia Sutherland as Lydia *in Balalaika* (1983), *Patricia* Lyle as Mei Li in *Flower Drum Song* (1982) and Deborah Lyons as Sarah Brown in *Guys and Dolls* (1986).

The last of these is worthy of special mention because, to date, she has performed no less than eighteen leading roles for the Society, with considerable aplomb. Certainly, in numerical terms, her portfolio ranks alongside those of Agnes Young and Jean Wintrope. As with the latter, her roles have been so varied that it is a case of choosing a favourite or all. They have all had something which has brought her public approbation.

Oklahoma rehearsal 1953 – St. John's Masonic Hall

FRONT ROW – (Prominent l-r) Walter Howarth, Cathie Little, Maisie Crozier, David Gibb, Ian Carruthers, John Kinghorn, Bill Tait (with handgun) Tom Hibbert, David Hobbs, Betty Howarth. Bert Armstrong, David Thomson and John Walsh (l-r) are just behind David Gibb.

At the BACK may be seen Jeanette Johnstone (white top) standing next to Louie Huggan. Ronnie Stormont (moustached) towers between Kitty Douglas and Rena Townsend. Evelyn Kersel and Pat Stormont are to the bottom left of the centrally hung picture. Ella Haig and Adam R. Hogg 2nd and 3rd from the right.

The Increasing Incorporation of Dance

The recurring theme of family connection in HAOS is a reminder that Deborah's parents, Jim and Kitty Hogarth (Douglas) were also in the Opera. The *Hawick Express* (12/3/57) dubbed him "the outstanding success of the 'new' boys" in *Love From Judy*, while the same newspaper (14/3/56) had written (of *Balalaika*) –

> "The play is notable, above all, for its dancing, and very outstanding was the fine performance by Kitty Douglas as the Countess."

Kitty, a model with Innes, Henderson (Braemar) knew a bit about movement; she was also following in the footsteps of Madge Gladstone and Cissie Aitken of the 'thirties and, more recently, Paula Ritchie, who had captivated the 1952 audiences with her portrayal of Azuri in *The Desert Song*, a role taken by Maureen Slorance in 1976. Since the early 'thirties, a dedicated dancing team, a kind of *corps de danse*, has been a recurring feature of the Society's productions. As the Society moved into the last quarter of its century, the popularity of shows with a greater number of principals and sub-principals saw dance fully integrated. If need be, everybody did everything where possible. But there has always been a place, if required, for the solo dance or the dance duo. Back in 1931, Eileen Barrie had been commended for her dancing skill. Vera Pringle and Ronnie Stormont did the honours in *Nina Rosa* (1953), but perhaps the most charismatic duo (and solo dancers) in the third quarter of the Society's history were James (Jimmy) Anderson and Anne Barker (later McCredie, now Anderson) who has now become a highly valued dance mistress and choreographer to HAOS and other societies. Their dream ballet work in *Oklahoma* (1967) raised the bar for all future productions. As well as dancing, this pair, over the years, have taken a wide variety of supporting parts.

As previously stated, the demands now made upon dancers would defy the wildest dreams of those who formed the dance troupes of even the 'fifties and 'sixties – in *Seven Brides For Seven Brothers* (1990) and *West Side Story* (1991) for example, in the rehearsals for which Keith McCredie, one of the 'Jets', suffered two fractured elbows, and Cameron Wright (of the same gang), a fractured leg. Dangerous stuff; nothing sissy about this!

Male Favourites of the Post-War Period to 1986

The late 'forties and early 'fifties also marked the Operatic debuts of Ian MacDonald and David Thomson (*A Country Girl* 1948), Ian Rorrison (*The New Moon* 1950), John Kinghorn (*The Desert Song* 1952),Tom Hibbert and William (Bill) Tait (*Nina Rosa* 1953) George Storie (*Pink Champagne* 1954), and Billy Jardine (*The Dancing Years* 1962). Two all too brief members from these years were Robert (Bert) Armstrong, who played five shows (1951-55) taking minor principal roles like Mindar in *The Desert Song* (1952), and his younger companion in so many other musical undertakings, David Gibb, who played two shows

(1955 and 1956), taking the role of Jud Fry in the former (*Oklahoma*).[40]

Rose Marie Mounties 1960
BACK – (l-r) Adam Hogg, Fred Duckworth, Jardine Handyside, Ian Carruthers.
MIDDLE – John Murphy, William Reid, William Renton, John Walsh, Ian MacDonald, John Kinghorn, Craig Spinks.
FRONT – Eric Burns, Walter Elder and William Robson.

The `shelf life` of at least two of these performers has been remarkable. Bill Tait was still playing a leading role (Adam, in *Seven Brides For Seven Brothers*) in 1990 before calling it a day as Doc in *West Side Story* a year later – an almost forty-year span of sterling service. Almost from his enrolment with the Society, Bill was awarded leading roles, his rich bass voice resonating in the far corners of the Town Hall. Among these were Jack Haines in *Nina Rosa* (1953), Eisenstein in *Pink Champagne* (1954), Leopold in *White Horse Inn* (1958), the Rev. Dishart in *Wild Grows The Heather* (1963), Joe in *Show Boat* (1972), Jigger in *Carousel* (1973) and Emile in *South Pacific* (1975). *Ol` Man River* and *Some Enchanted Evening* will always evoke memories of Bill Tait in Hawick. Bill died at the end of 2006.

---

[40] Both were awarded the MBE in 2002 for services to the community. Bert Armstrong was Official Hawick Common-Riding Song Singer 1973-84 inclusive.

George Storie has been no less prolific. Joining the Society in 1953, George has distinguished himself in many roles, among them Jim Kenyon in *Rose Marie* (1960), Carl (with his wife, Rita, as female lead, Sarah) in *Bitter Sweet* (1966), Billy Bigelow in *Carousel* (1973), Red Shadow in *The Desert Song* (1976) and Emile in *South Pacific* (1985). One could go on. He was still treading the boards as Arvide Abernathy in *Guys And Dolls* in 2002.

Opera Men – Three Presidents – Ian MacDonald, John Forrest, John Walsh.

In such listings it would be remiss not to recognise those who have caught the public imagination in one or two shows. These include Elliot Kyle as Robert in *The New Moon* (1950), Ian Carruthers as Captain Paul Fontaine and the inimitable David Hobbs as Benjamin Kidd in *The Desert Song* (1952) and as Ali Hakim in *Oklahoma* (1955), Tom Hibbert as Will Parker in the same production, John Kinghorn as Charlie Davenport in *Annie Get Your Gun* (1959), Ian MacDonald as Dvorak in *Summer Song* (1960), Eddie Hill as Danilo in *The Merry Widow*(1965), Ronnie Bald (Frank Butler in *Annie Get Your Gun* – 1959, Hard Boiled Herman in *Rose Marie* – 1960, and the King in *The King And I* – 1964), Bill Renton as Jud Fry (*Oklahoma* – 1967), Eric Burns (Ali Hakim in *Oklahoma* – 1967), Wallace Shaw (Professor Higgins in *My Fair Lady* – 1969), Gerry Nixon as Freddie Eynsford Hill in the same show, Stewart Frame (Captain von Trapp in *The Sound Of Music* – 1971); David Crowe (Enoch Snow in *Carousel* – 1973), Peter Anderson (Captain Paul Fontaine in *The Desert Song* – 1976), Edward Martin (the King in *The King And I* – 1979) and Billy Jardine (Curly in *Oklahoma* – 1967 and Sky Masterson in *Guys And Dolls* – 1986). This listing is no more than representative, because these people were in many shows at differing levels of involvement.

And then there is the army of supporting part holders whose characterisations are equally valid – men like John Walsh, Tom Shearman, Jimmy Anderson, Kenneth Ellis, Wat Elder, Bill Renton, Tom Murdoch, Jardine Handyside, Jimmy Murray, Andy Gaston, Norman Graham, Addie Robson, David Peacock, Bill Robson, Ronnie Stormont, Billy Byers,[41] Walter Howarth, Fred Duckworth, John Forrest, George Milligan, Keith Robertson and Jim Wallace; women like Sybil Storie, Maisie Ormiston (Crozier), Morag Murphy (Smith), Evelyn Kersel, Dorothy Palmer Douglas, Netta Fulton, Wilma Waters, Maureen Black (Smith), Anne Scott, Moira Stewart (Fleming) and Eileen Aitkin (Scott), and Patricia Esslemont (now Adam). This is the stuff of a successful society.

Husband and wife leads – George and Rita Storie
Bitter Sweet 1966

The Return of Frances Davis 1951-1957

Of all the producers experienced by HAOS up to the second coming of Jean Wintrope in 1989, none had so profound an effect upon the psyche of the members as Frances Davis. She was the consummate stage director, interpreting not only the author`s directions in the libretto but also arranging the dances. A report in *Hawick News* (17/12/1936) ascribed to Miss. Davis "an easy and pleasant manner which should do much to make everyone feel `at home` on the stage." As may be, but those who recall this little woman recall someone of boundless energy with a core of steel. She had first come to Hawick at the end of 1936 to produce *The Student Prince* and remained with the company until the outbreak of the War. She had experienced an eventful war, having been torpedoed in the Mediterranean Sea while voyaging to entertain troops in the Near East. Her rescue by a destroyer was fortuitous for the companies like HAOS which had forged such a good working relationship with her; all of which brought to her an added *cachet*. As HAOS discovered, after the War, she was difficult to get, but her six years with the post-War company was an experience that few of its members would forget, not least, aspiring producers. All was assiduously rehearsed to the finest detail and her word was the law, a position which a grateful Society willingly accorded her, but one which, when assumed by future producers, occasionally discomfited

---

[41] Billy Byers later became a stage manager for London productions such as Agatha Christie`s *The Mousetrap*.

56

Golden Jubilee Celebrations – Full Company 1960

BACK ROW - (l-r) Eric Burns, William Reid, Walter Elder, John Kinghorn, George Storie, William Renton, Peter Horne, Craig Spinks, Ian Crawford, James Anderson, William Robson.

SECOND ROW – Nan Anderson, Netta Scott, Nancy Aitken, Jan Blackwood, May Matthews, Margaret Logan, Patricia Hogg, Margaret Peden, Adam Hogg, Margaret Mather, Vera Mundell, Moira Fleming, Moyra Farquharson, June Robson, Margaret Sullivan, Myra Russell, Rene Townsend.

THIRD ROW – Brenda Whyte, Christine Hill, Ann Bidmead, Irene Cowen, Maisie Ormiston, Elizabeth Warwick, Eileen Scott, Rita Storie, Jean Wintrope, Maimie Johnstone, Jaqueline Scott, Betty Burnet, John Walsh.

FRONT ROW – John Forrest (Hon. Treasurer), W.A. Deans Ellis (Hon. Chorus Master), Louie Huggan, Adam Aitken, William D. Turnbull, Ian W. Carruthers (Vice President), Robert Wilson (Hon. President), Ian R. MacDonald (President), Eleanor Dalgleish (Hon. President), Tom E. Shortreed (Hon. President), H. Grenville Morgan (Hon. Joint Secretary), Fred Duckworth (Hon. Joint Secretary), Ella Haig (Hon. Patron Secretary), David O. Stothart. Unable to be present were Betty A. Wilson, Nan Whillans, Evelyn Lancaster, Diana Harper, Ada Robson, Maureen Black, Betty Howarth, Margaret Galloway, Eric Whitehead (Hon. Guest Conductor), Edward Hill, Tom Huggan, John Murphy, Oliver Combe.

musical directors. At Hawick Town Hall she had to produce in what many, even at that time, would have regarded as intolerable conditions, but she was sufficiently professional to see these as a challenge to be overcome rather than as an impediment to achievement. Her work became a yardstick by which those whom she directed would measure the efficacy of all future producers.

Founder Members at Golden Jubilee Dinner, November, 1960

(l-r) – Ina Johnstone (née Turnbull), John M. Ballantyne, Agnes Stewart,
Helen M. Whillans (née Charters), Sarah Armstrong, Adam M. Aitken and Jean Gladstone.

Passing The Baton

The long stage careers of such as Ian Carruthers, Bill Tait and George Storie serve to bring overlap in the generations of amateur operatic enthusiasts. The baton, to use a metaphor for experience, is handed on. So Bill Tait began in a stage pairing with Jean Wintrope in 1952-53 with Frances Davis as Producer and partnered Deborah Lyons in his penultimate year (1990) with Jean Wintrope as Producer. Indeed, the same could be said of Jean`s accrued experience as principal and Producer extending up to 2008 – sixty years. A society cannot put a price on this, which is one reason why it must cater for the full age range when choosing its shows rather than being influenced only by `what the young ones want.` The history of HAOS demonstrates that, naturally, many of the young ones, for various reasons, usually marriage and removal, leave the Society after only a year or two. The Opera today operates in a far more nomadic society than when it was founded in 1910. Age-related departure from the stage is an inevitability, but generational overlap, or `stranding`, is the strength of the Society.

The King And I 1964

Ross Taylor (Louis), Jean Wintrope (Anna), Jean Rorrison (Lady Thiang), Bill Renton (The Kralahome),
Ronnie Bald (The King), Billy Jardine (Prince Chulalongkorn), Vera Mundell (Tuptim).

Similar is the case of comedy. Perhaps, in the annals of HAOS, there has never been anyone quite like David Stothart (though David Hobbs was pretty good at it as well), but the same could be said of Sandy Herd, who joined the Society in 1962 and was the fount of mirth for three and a half decades until his death in 1997 at the lamentably early age of fifty four. Comedy is so much part and parcel of any successful musical. The librettist may write the lines, but it is the manner and timing of delivery which bring the laughs and set an audience alight. Herd`s sense of timing was, like Stothart`s, flawless, and some of the parts he played allowed him full scope for the expression of an undeniable gift – for example, as Max in *The Sound of Music* (1971), Billis in *South Pacific* (1975), Benjamin Kidd (does every society`s favourite comedian get this part?) in *The Desert Song* (1976), Nathan Detroit in *Guys And Dolls* (1986), or as a gangster in *Kiss Me, Kate* (1989). But, like Stothart, Herd could turn in a more serious characterisation if required and, again, as with Stothart, when Sandy Herd stepped on to the stage, spontaneous glee and a *frisson* of expectancy permeated the auditorium.

Wild Grows The Heather 1963 Principals

BACK ROW – Douglas Gray, Billy Reid, John Walsh, Jean Rorrison, Jean Wintrope, Bill Tait, Bill Renton, Jimmy Anderson, Bill Robson, Brenda Whyte. MIDDLE – (standing) Betty Howarth. FRONT ROW – Ian MacDonald, Billy Jardine, Christine Lyon, Eric Burns.

Wild Grows The Heather 1963 Women`s Chorus

STANDING – (l-r) May Matthews, Wilma Waters, Margaret Logan, Elsie Mitchell, June Little,
Moira Fleming, Margery Nichol, Margot Scott, Rena Townsend, Nancy Aitken.
SEATED – Kathleen Watson, Eleanor Delgatty, Maureen Black, Christine Crawford, Margaret Sullivan, ? .

The Merry Widow 1965 Principals

BACK – (l-r) Eddie Hill, John Bamforth, Ian MacDonald, Fred Duckworth, Billy Jardine, Ian Carruthers, Jimmy Anderson, Bill Renton, Eric Burns. FRONT - Wilma Waters, Eileen Smith, Jean Wintrope, Jean Rorrison, Brenda Walker.

Bitter Sweet 1966 – Chorus in action

CENTRAL LINE-UP – (l-r) Eric Burns, Elsie Mitchell, Christine Crawford, Kathryn Scott, Morag Murphy, Eileen Aitkin, Janette Huggan, Pat Murray, Wilma Waters, Joe Oliver, Myra McLeod, Bill Renton. Margery Nichol and Jimmy Anderson front right. Ian Carruthers, Jardine Handyside and Ian MacDonald in second row left. Rena Townsend and Eddie Hill in background right.

Post Card Girls from *Oklahoma* 1967
Pat Hogg, Pat Murray, Eileen Aitkin, Brenda Walker

Wild Violets 1968 – Principals
BACK – (l-r) Maureen Black, Myra McLeod, Dorothy Palmer Douglas, Francis Cannon, Neil Smith, Ian Carruthers,
Pat Lyle, Jardine Handyside, Adam Robson, Maisie Ormiston, Forbes Gray. MIDDLE (SEATED l-r) – Gerry Nixon, Brenda Walker,
Billy Jardine, Rita Storie, Sandy Herd, Morag Murphy. FRONT – Peter Ormiston.

The Sound Of Music 1971 – Children and peasants

(l-r) VERY BACK – Louise Bookless, Eleanor McVittie. BACK – George Storie, Alison Ford, Dorothy Scott, Jim Anderson, Alison Seeley, Bill Robson, Anne Wintrope, Billy Byers.
MIDDLE – Brenda Walker, Liz Smith, Maureen Slorance, Janette McGregor, Pat Murray, Shelagh Kinghorn.
FRONT – (Children) Anne Barker, Sandra Brown, Kim (John) Elliot, Ruth Nichols, Brian Walker, Sybil Wintrope, Deborah Hogarth.

My Fair Lady 1969 – Ladies` Chorus with Eliza

BACK – (l-r) Maureen Black, Alison Ford, Pat Murray, Kathryn Scott, June Little. MIDDLE – Maisie Hill, Letta Dalgleish, Jean Wintrope (Eliza), Maisie Ormiston, Morag Murphy. FRONT – Moira Oliver, Elsie Mitchell.

Show Boat 1972 – Principals

(l-r) BACK – Bill Robson, David Crowe, Jimmy Anderson, Bill Tait, George Storie, Stewart Frame, Billy Byers. MIDDLE – Maisie Ormiston, Anne Barker, Sandy Herd, Myra McLeod, Jean Wintrope. FRONT – Alison Seeley.

Carousel 1973 – Principals

(l-r) BACK – Letta Dalgleish, David Crowe, Sally Robson, Bill Tait, Alison Seeley.
MIDDLE – Billy Byers, Brenda Walker, George Storie, Andy Gaston. FRONT – Anne McCredie.

South Pacific 1975

(l-r) Letta Dalgleish (Nellie Forbush),
Lynn Gilchrist (Ngana),
Bill Tait (Emile de Becque),
Ian Dickson (Jerome).

South Pacific 1975 – Ladies` Chorus

BACK (l-r) Julie Barker, Janette McGregor, Maureen Slorance, Liz Smith, Anne McCredie, Jayne Black. MIDDLE – Eileen Aitken, Myra Mcleod, Marion Mallin. FRONT – Marianne Smith, Alison Ford, Pat Esslemont, Sybil Laidlaw, Edith Hogg, Moira Stewart. FOREGROUND (left) Pat Lyle, (right) Morag Murphy.

Call Me Madam 1977 – Jim Wallace (Cosmo) with two times Mrs. Sally Adams

The Producer, Elizabeth Seton, felt that the female leading role was too taxing to sustain over a week, so it was shared by Christine Lyon (left) and Rita Storie (right).

'Never work with children and animals on stage!' *White Horse Inn* 1974

BACK (l-r) Norma Dalgleish, Sandra Brown, Shirley Murray, Marianne Smith, Moira Stewart, Gail Anderson, Jacqueline Scott, Ruth Nichols.

FRONT – Adrienne Thompson, Rosalie Thompson, Susan Scott.

The goats were Napoleon and Josephine and belonged to Mrs. Smith (pictured) and her husband Rob, in practice locally as a vet.

The Desert Song 1976 – Ladies' Chorus

(l-r) BACK – Janice Dunshea, Carol Murray, Marianne Smith.
MIDDLE – Eileen Aitkin, Dorothy McCredie, Pat Aitchison, Marion Mallin, Liz Armstrong, Joyce Robson, Edith Hogg, Julie Barker.
FRONT – June Little, Moira Stewart, Alison Ford, Dorothy Palmer Douglas, Alison Seeley, Wendy Hough, Pat Lyle.

The Desert Song 1976 – Legionnaires

(l-r) Fred Duckworth, Gerald Murray, Jack Middlemass, James Murray, Andy Gaston, Norman Graham.
Jim Wallace, Alan Hughes, Ian Carruthers, Graham Morrison, Peter Anderson (Captain Paul Fontaine).

The Desert Song 1976

(l-r) STANDING – Sandy Herd, David Crowe, George Milligan, Dorothy Palmer Douglas, Eddie Martin, Letta Dalgleish.
SEATED – Peter Anderson, Maureen Slorance (Azuri), George Brown.

Call Me Madam 1977 – Ladies` Chorus

(l-r) BACK – Muriel Graham, Myra McLeod, Pat Aitchison, Margaret Slorance, Alison Seeley, Wendy Scott, Alison Ford.
MIDDLE – June Little, Moira Stewart, Pat Esslemont, Eileen Aitkin. FRONT – Marion Mallin, Margery Brown,
Carol Murray, Edith Hogg, Morag Murphy.

Bless The Bride 1978 – The Willow Family

(l-r) BACK – Marion Mallin, Eileen Aitkin, Deborah Hogarth, Myra McLeod, Alison Seeley.
FRONT – Janette McGregor, Sally Robson, Eddie Martin, Morag Murphy.

The King And I 1979

Christine Lyon (Anna), Billy Jardine (Prince Chulalongkorn) and Sally Robson (Lady Thiang) with the King's children.

CHILDREN – (l-r) BACK – Jill Matthews, Ruth Murray, Graham Slorance, Fiona McGregor, Morag Dickson, Lesley Grey, Morag Robertson, Katrina Jackson. MIDDLE (l-r) – Andrea Turnbull, Noelle Murphy, Leah Slorance, Karen Little, Jane Broatch, Alison Lauder.
FRONT – (l-r) Diane Stewart, Kerry Slorance, Donna Mackie, Craig McCredie, Karen Mackie, Louise Brown, Melanie Seeley.

Chapter VII

READJUSTMENT IN THE THIRD QUARTER

All societies and clubs wax and wane; that is the nature of them, and in this respect HAOS has also undergone periods of uncertainty. Notwithstanding some memorable individual stage performances, the `seventies and early `eighties were, generally speaking, difficult years for the Society, the culmination of which was its inability, in 1980, to present a show. The problem, ostensibly, was one of attracting men to the Society for that year`s choice – *Fiddler On The Roof.* But , in truth, some of the shows leading up to this particular crisis had been `hanging by an eyebrow` and occasionally it was the talent of one or two particular performers that pulled them through, for example, George Storie as Red Shadow in *The Desert Song* (1976). Indeed, to be able to present that show, the Society had to approach a former member, Peter Anderson (who had moved to Innerleithen), to get them out of a tight spot by agreeing to take the part of Captain Paul Fontaine. Another indicator of the Society`s ambivalence during this period may be seen in the accompaniment for *South Pacific* (1985). The `orchestra` consisted of only two pianos and an electronic organ – no percussion whatsoever. While there is nothing wrong with this (it may even have brought benefits), it seemed a far cry from the Opera`s more sumptuous days.

Mid - `Sixties Opera Dinner
TABLE FARSIDE – Betty Howarth, Betty Burnet, Eleanor Dalgleish, Adam Hogg, Rena Townsend.
NEARSIDE – John Walsh, Dorothy Walsh, May Matthews, Jim Matthews and Ella Haig.
Anne Hutton, June Little and Elsie Mitchell (partially obscured) are in the background with Jim Little (centre) facing out.

Generally speaking, the Society`s best years have been those during which there has been stability in either production or musical direction, preferably both. Between 1969 and 1979, the Society had five different Musical Directors – David Griffiths, Mary D. Rowell, Betty Scott, David Young and Basil Deane. With such flux and continual adjustment to different methods of working, confidence and trust are undermined, uncertainty created and basic company discipline (essential to the final product) crumbles. In the same decade, there were four different producers – Phyllis Ward, Tommy McIntyre, Elizabeth Seton and Jean Wintrope, all with their individual idiosyncracies and requirements as to application and attendance.

Opera Dinner, King`s Hotel – 1976

(l-r) TABLE FARSIDE – Elizabeth Cavers, Pat Aitchison, Hugh McLeod, Myra McLeod, Alison Seeley, Jim Aitkin.
NEARSIDE – (l-r) Dorothy McCredie, Kenneth McCredie, Ian Seeley, Jim Stewart. Bill Renton in background behind Hugh McLeod.

In the real world, outwith amateur operatics, television had taken an incalculable toll on active participation in anything, but markedly so on theatre and cinema attendance. In Hawick the political fall-out from Ted Heath`s confrontation with the miners in 1972 and the resulting three-day working week, extended or altered work shifts to combat power cuts and the need to be `flexible`, played havoc with an older concept of commitment. People, generally, were less willing to be tied down. In the `seventies, Secretary Nancy Aitken continued to keep a record of attendance. By the `eighties, such procedure would be considered demeaning and unnecessary.

Added to this, the generation which had survived the War and that which had re-started the Society in the `Brave New World` which followed it were becoming thin on the ground. The misguided notion among many males in Hawick that stage work isn`t a `man thing` (this also affects male church attendance) was also symptomatic of a different way of thinking to the likes of John M. Ballantyne, who had no problem about his operatic connection and could still be President of `the Greens`, or Scottish rugby internationalist W.E. Kyle who had regularly `trodden the boards` in Edwardian times. Men who didn`t feel the need to follow the herd were scarce and sufficient numbers could not be rallied to sustain the projected performance of *Fiddler On The Roof*. The break, when it came in 1980, saw the departure of Nancy Aitken as Secretary, and the Treasurer of long standing, John Forrest, called it a day two years later. 1982 and 1984 saw the deaths of the last surviving founder members – Etta Guy, at the age of ninety seven and John Miller Ballantyne at the age of ninety four respectively.

The Pajama Game 1981 – Dance Tableau

(l-r) BACK – Anne McCredie. MIDDLE – Pat Aitchison, Norma Stewart, Pat Lyle, Roger Storie, Ron Smith, Billy Chisholm, Janette McGregor, Maureen Slorance. FRONT – Anita Brandon, Liz Armstrong.

These were clearly uncertain times for the Society, yet when practices resumed, somewhat falteringly, in1980 for *The Pajama Game*, it was to be the start of another round of four different producers and five different musical directors up to the seventy fifth anniversary celebrations in 1985-86. `Celebrations` may be something of an overstatement. Seventy Fifth Anniversary Concerts on 28th, 29th and 30th October, 1985, arranged by Jean Wintrope, with Ian MacDonald as compère, though reasonably well attended, received polite approbation from loyal HAOS followers, but they were unenthusiastically reported, with little detail of individual

The Pajama Game 1981 – Rag trade workers
(l-r) BACK – Eileen Aitkin, Edith Hogg, Alison Seeley, Moira Stewart, Pat Sutherland, June Little, Wilma Waters.
FRONT – Moira Boyd, Anne Cockburn.

Flower Drum Song 1982
Pat Aitchison, Janette McGregor, Rita Storie, Maureen Slorance, Anne Clark

Balalaika 1983 – Full Cast

BACK - *?* , *?* , Deborah Lyons, Sandra Smart, Derek Fraser, Tony Lewis, Jimmy Murray, Drew Gibb.

MIDDLE – Pat Esslemont, Rosemarie Watt, Letta Dalgleish, Myra McLeod, Eddie Martin, Keith Robertson, Wilma Watters, Jim Wallace, Pat Sutherland, Morag Murphy, Sandy Herd, Iain Carruthers, Christine Lyon, Ron Smith, Alison Seeley, Edith Hogg, Linda Kyle, Margaret Horne.

FRONT – Jennifer Smart, Noelle Murphy, Rosalie Thompson, Alison Horne, Janette McGregor, Anne Clark, Pat Lyle, Anne McCredie, Sally Robson.

The Sound Of Music 1984 – Captain`s Children
(l-r) BACK – Alan Storie, Craig McCredie, Andrea Munro, Leah Slorance.
CENTRE - Rosalie Thompson. FRONT – Melanie Seeley, Louise Brown.

items. There appears to have been no celebratory photograph taken of the Society at this point in its history. It was, perhaps, symptomatic of a more general atmosphere of disorientation, malaise and lack of positivity. The Society was in need of a breath of fresh air, and that duly arrived in 1985 with the appointment of Bill Harvey, a policeman by profession and a keen amateur Thespian associated with the Innerleithen and District Operatic Society, as Producer.

HAOS Seventy-fifth Anniversary Concert
(l-r) - Bill Tait, Billy Jardine and George Storie strut their stuff.

Chapter VIII

THE FINAL QUARTER

The Approach To The Millennium And On To The Centenary

Bill Harvey's avuncular bonhomie and gregariousness engendered a sense of common purpose among male and female Society members alike. The show chosen for 1986, *Guys And Dolls*, could not have been better for the Society at this time because it allowed for the cultivation of a vibrant male contingent. It is a tuneful, tight-knit, sardonic yet funny show with a real zippy `showbiz` feel. From the moment the orchestra strikes up *I`ve Never Been In Love Before* at the beginning of the overture, a sense of expectation of good things to come is engendered. And the Hawick audience wasn`t disappointed. Here were Billy Jardine, Sandy Herd, Deborah Lyons and Rita Storie giving sharp, engaging performances, supported by a host of `characters` who played their parts

Guys And Dolls 1986
Brian Leslie, Peter Robertson and Alfie Storie

with *élan*. Numbers like *A Bushel And A Peck, If I Were A Bell, Sue Me, Luck Be A Lady, Sit Down, You`re Rocking The Boat* and, of course, *I`ve Never Been In Love Before* make this show a winner – and it was a winner at Hawick for Bill Harvey and the Society. From this point on, although Bill Harvey did only four shows, the Society`s credit rose over the following two decades to encompass some of the most ambitious musicals in the repertoire.

Bill`s approach and personality brought some redress to the `man thing` problem and it is notable that, with his coming, the Society acquired a corps of good, reliable men whose unashamed commitment pointed the way for others. These were Peter Robertson, an instructor at the Katherine Elliot Centre and his colleague Les Sneddon, and electrician Steve Treacy. Brian Leslie, a former naval officer, had joined the previous year and Stuart Gibson, a promising amateur footballer, joined the following year, 1986. All of them were to take on significant roles in the years ahead, Les leading as Edvard Grieg in *Song Of Norway* (1988) and as Fred Graham/Petruchio in *Kiss Me, Kate* (1989). Brian was adept in humorous roles, taking the part of the hapless henpecked Count in the former and that of a gangster (*Brush Up Your Shakespeare*) in the latter. He became President of the Society between 1989

Guys And Dolls 1986
Billy Jardine with Sandy Herd under pressure

and 1995, but was tragically killed in a road accident in November, 1995 at the age of only 48 – a huge loss to the Society. Peter and Steve, over the following two decades, gave sterling service in numerous supporting parts and in the chorus. Of Brian, more later. The Society seemed to be going forward once again.

Bill Harvey`s approach also freed up the actual management of the presentation of all future shows. Until his arrival, there was a distinct operational hierarchy which probably had its origins in the heyday of Frances Davis when the Producer was `God` and the programmes carried the legend – "Entire Production Under The Direction Of ----." It was an announcement which, over the years, irked several musical directors who, in spite of the vast amount of input they had invested in a show, were made to feel like mere functionaries whose valid opinions could be overruled at a producer`s whim.

In Bill`s second production – *Half A Sixpence* – the Society experienced difficulties in getting a Musical Director and Ian Seeley, then Head of Music at Hawick High School was approached. Seeley, however, had been involved with the Opera orchestra since 1973, in various capacities – pianist, organist and double bass player, and had observed at first hand the dynamics in the relationships between producer, musical director and choreographer. He

79

Half A Sixpence 1987
Jim Arbon as the eccentric Chitterlow

had been less than impressed and was reluctant to accept the position of Musical Director unless some fundamental changes in the working relationship with the Producer could be renegotiated and ratified by the Committee. Bill Harvey, generous to a fault, readily agreed. "Entire Production Under The Direction Of ..." was consigned to history and replaced by "Production Team" with the component directors having equal say in presentation, auditions, etc. and an equal right to full consultation in matters affecting the production. Having regard to the pressures of his work in the High School, Seeley agreed to do one year as M.D. In the event, he did two.

Seeley`s schoolteacherly approach may not, at the time, have suited all; initially, some may have stayed away. But there was nothing unreasonable in starting a practice at an agreed time, or notifying the Producer, Musical Director

or Choreographer that you could not be present for a particular practice. (As pianist to the Society he had seen how *laissez faire* could wreak havoc with rehearsals and the time of other participants in a dramatic group or dance sequence be squandered). It wasn`t so much about rules as about mutual respect between fellow participants. If a practice was arranged to start at 7.30 p.m. or any other time, that now was exactly when it started and this was agreed in advance with the company. Whatever the perception, the Harvey-Seeley-Cleland team worked well and confirmed

Half A Sixpence 1987
(l-r) Brian Leslie, Ian McKenzie, Stuart Gibson and Elliot Goldie. This was Elliot`s first leading role as Kipps. It was also Stuart Gibson`s stage debut.

Ladies` Chorus – *Half A Sixpence* 1987

(l-r) BACK – Pat Esslemont, Linsay Sanger, Anne Gillespie, Julie Storie, Linda Kyle, Margaret Horne, Karen Lawson.
FRONT – Vanessa Storie, Rosemarie Watt, Alison Seeley, Elizabeth Crowe.

the value of the new team approach to production.

Their first collaborative effort was to be David Heneker`s *Half A Sixpence,* an unpretentious English music theatre piece with good melodies and an uncomplicated story line. Song and dance numbers like *If The Rain`s Got to Fall,* and *Flash, Bang, Wallop* and the boy-meets-girl thing in the title song and wistful waltz number *She`s Too Far Above Me* seemed to take a trick with cast and audience alike. The principals, Anne Clark, Elliot Goldie and Jim Arbon, a highly popular team within a company which now seemed at one with itself, made for a very happy show. It smacked of what a former President of the `thirties, John Campbell, called "good clean entertainment." In spite of all this, the company was fully stretched to mount this show. There were no spares and almost everyone in it had lines to say, but the seeds of change had been sown and, in a sublime act of faith, the Society chose *Song Of Norway* for 1988. In terms of difficulty, *Song Of Norway* was several notches above *Half A Sixpence*, but it had everything the Society required to build confidence – chorus work a-plenty, challenging solos and concerted numbers, colourful dance sequences and scope for children`s participation – always an audience puller.

Half A Sixpence 1987

Flash,Bang,Wallop Wedding Line-up

(l-r) Brian Leslie, Stuart Gibson, Ian McKenzie, Elliot Goldie, Anne Clark,
Alison Seeley, Elizabeth Crowe, Vanessa Storie, Rosemarie Watt.

The Opera Orchestra 1987

Three musical directors* of the Society are present. (l-r) Graham Borthwick, Betty Scott,* David Watson,
Jeffrey Rimmer, Edward Ferguson,* Robert Waddell, Lynn Jeary, Ian Seeley* (Conductor), Peter Chamberlain (leader),
Alex Wands. Obscured are Louise Matthew, Charles Maynes and William Drummond.

The production team had their work cut out. The orchestral score presented Seeley with conducting challenges to be met in only two rehearsals, not the least of his problems being the incorporation of an abridged version of Grieg`s Piano Concerto in A Minor which forms the grand finale to the piece. This is also choreographed and there is an off-stage chorus at the very end. What is not often realised by audiences is that the Opera orchestra, or `band`, may have only one full rehearsal together – something at which even full-time professionals might baulk. This `band call` precedes the Dress Rehearsal which, in turn, allows the orchestra a second run through. Nevertheless, the latter is a `first` in terms of accompanying the players on stage. Pressure!

Song Of Norway 1988
Anne McCredie dances Adelina, prima ballerina, in a showdown with Louisa (Hazel Devlin).
(l-r) Pat Esslemont, Ian McKenzie, Alison Seeley (semi-obscured), Deborah Lyons, Rita Storie (semi-obscured),
Jim Arbon, Sandy Herd, Brian Leslie and Hazel Devlin.

Song Of Norway, as a theatrical piece, has been dubbed a `turkey` (i.e. unsuccessful) by some critics in the wider musical world, but the Hawick production attracted audiences from all over the Borders and beyond. It is not a term to which most of those who took part in it would subscribe. Indeed, many look back on this show with real affection. For the Society, however, it established a new level of aspiration and confidence. It also attracted people from other Border towns to join the Hawick Society.

Song Of Norway 1988

Freddie (Stuart Gibson) strikes up his fiddle for some national dancing

Some of the children here became Opera stalwarts. They are (l-r) Alistair Thompson, Craig McCredie, Iain Scott, Tanya Slorance, Lyndsey McCredie and Adele Slorance. Familiar faces behind include (l-r) Linsay Sanger, Cameron Wright, Pat Rolland, Karen Lawson, Letta Dalgleish, Sandy Herd, Lesley Stormont, Myra McLeod, Margaret Blacklock, Jim Arbon, Zilla Oddy, Rita Storie, Rona Young, Alison Seeley, Margaret Horne, Elliot Goldie, Julie Storie (obscured), Anne Gillespie, Pat Lyle and Ian McKenzie.

In order to boost numbers for the sumptuous chorus work of *Song Of Norway*, Bill Harvey encouraged an entourage from Galashiels and its environs to travel with him to Hawick. One of these, Hazel Devlin, eventually carried the female leading role of Louisa with a panache that elicited both envy and admiration from her peers. Other `pailmerks` were in evidence in that show and the `Gala Brigade` were, for the following decade, welcomed into the Society as honorary Teries. One of them, Jane Headspeath, a niece of Letta Dalgleish and Myra McLeod (former principals in *South Pacific* and *The Desert Song)* became HAOS`s President over the two years embracing the 1996 and 1997 shows. Derek Calder, a Galashiels music teacher who joined the Society in 1991, eventually became Musical Director.

The 1995-1996 season saw the philosophy of Irving Berlin`s famous number *There`s No Business Like Show Business*, from *Annie, Get Your Gun,* tested to the limit. Brian Leslie was killed in a road accident in November, 1995, the Society`s pianist, Mary Rowell, developed appendicitis prior to the dress rehearsal and, on the Friday of the week of the show (*Show*

Boat), Steve Treacy`s twenty-one year old son died in a road accident in Peeblesshire. Niall Bailey, a talented High School pupil who was to have been the on-stage accompanist for Julie`s solo *Bill*, was redeployed to the orchestra and Steve`s part (Pete) was taken, for the final three performances, by Frank Barker. "And so," in Berlin`s memorable words, " on with the show!" Notwithstanding the tsunami of emotion engulfing them, the cast went on with grit and determination to present a show as worthy as any in the Society`s history, not only for Hawick, but for Steve.

The final quarter of the Society`s first hundred years has been marked by productions of a standard unimagined even in the post-War years. Improvements to Hawick Town Hall back in the winter of 1964-65, including a new sound and public address system, were a seismic shift in terms

Kiss Me, Kate 1989
Les Sneddon with Hazel Devlin

Kiss Me, Kate 1989
Brush Up Your Shakespeare
Gangsters Sandy Herd and Brian Leslie

of what the Society (and the Hawick public) had endured since well before the Second World War but, from the Opera`s point of view, did not go far enough. Although audience comfort and ancillary services like a kitchen, cloakrooms, lesser hall and bar were provided, dressing room facilities, to this day, remain primitive and, at best, spartan. The stage remained inadequate for the satisfactory movement of large choruses and there was no proper orchestra pit in spite of considerable basement depth being available under the stage and in front of it (the former police cells). In any future development, these, and the provision of moveable tiered seating in the area, would seem to be priorities. To have the blast of a horn or trombone in your ear because you have paid for a front row seat is no great privilege!

Kiss Me, Kate 1989

CENTRE STAGE (l-r) Les Sneddon, Hazel Devlin, Dorothy Meechan and Elliot Goldie (Petruchio, Katherine, Bianca and Lucento)

At the behest of Jean Wintrope, who had followed Bill Harvey as Producer in 1989, the Society tackled the first of the latter problems by commissioning a bespoke, moveable and storable stage extension. The beneficial effect on production was immediate. Sound was no longer lost in the great spatial void behind the proscenium and there was space for movement that Frances Davis would have died for. In the `nineties, the concept of a `live stage` continued to develop with the wider use of increasingly sophisticated body and head microphones. The days of amazement when Jean Turnbull`s "every word reached the crowded galleries" (as *Rio Rita* – 1949) were long gone. If you don`t  have a large, well-produced voice like Jean Turnbull`s, you can still, today, be an Opera principal.

The level of expectation in dance had also been jacked up by the ever-pervasive influence of the entertainment media, but the appointment of Rhona Cleland for the Society`s 1982 show (*Flower Drum Song*) introduced a wholly novel and energetic approach to chorus choreography which the members found stimulating and positive. Rhona worked her magical powers with the company until 2003 when she was succeeded by Hawick`s own highly competent and experienced Anne Anderson (née Barker). Rhona`s twenty one years with the Society brought that special mixture of security, trust and mutual respect which grows to the advantage of a company.

Similar was Jean Wintrope`s nineteen-show run as Producer, commencing in 1989. Jean had previously produced for the Society in 1978, 1979, 1982 and 1983. She came to the producer`s chair with a personal experience of amateur dramatic and operatic roles arguably

Seven Brides For Seven Brothers 1990
Deborah Lyons (Milly) with Bill Tait (Adam) in his last leading role

Seven Brides For Seven Brothers 1990

(l-r) Steve Treacy	Stuart Learmonth	Stuart Gibson	Elliot Goldie	Neil Comely	Les Sneddon
Kathryn Cockburn	Anne McCredie	Anne Clark	Melanie Seeley	Lesley Stormont	Dorothy Meechan

unrivalled in the South of Scotland (and probably even wider) and, as she relaunched herself with the Society in 1989 for *Seven Brides For Seven Brothers* (1990), it soon became apparent that her grip on all stage matters was a dynamic one. For all her experience, Jean`s tenure as Producer always allowed for her own continued development. It was on an ever upward curve and, as a result of her philosophy, so was the work of HAOS.

The musical direction component of the `production team` continued to be protean, but remarkable standards were achieved, particularly under the direction of Chris Achenbach, James Letham and Derek Calder. Chris`s formidable keyboard skills ensured that virtually no musical need be outwith the ambit of the Society and this was probably best demonstrated in *West Side Story* (1991). Jim Letham is one of the most consummate musicians ever to have worked in the Scottish Borders. His skills as pianist, conductor and composer are of a calibre which might challenge the best in his profession. He followed Ian Seeley at Hawick High School and the energy and enthusiasm he has displayed there have attracted favourable comment throughout the region. Apart from his undeniable musical competency, Derek Calder has brought something extra to HAOS as M.D. Stage musicals are his hobby and his passion. He has loved directing them, he has revelled in being on stage in them, and what he

`The Angels` (*Anything Goes*) 1992
(l-r) Anne McCredie, Kathryn Wilson, Dorothy Meechan and Maureen Slorance with leading lady, Deborah Lyons (Reno)

doesn`t know about them isn`t worth knowing. He has been Musical Director since 2002 and, in similar fashion to Jean Wintrope, is ever willing to excel anything he has done previously. With each ensuing year he, like Jean, has increased his influence on the Society`s performances. With such talented forces at work with the Society, the reasons behind the successes of the final quarter can readily be understood. The other essential ingredients of these successes are, of course, the people on the stage and their very individual talents. A Producer such as a Davis or Wintrope or any of the M.D.s mentioned may mould and train, but gold will not be made from straw, no matter their expertise.

The Company in 1992

(l-r) BACK ROW – Jim Wallace, Frank Barker, Steve Treacy, Craig McCredie, Des Devine, Nick Rosanno, Brian Leslie, Graham Coulson.
THIRD ROW – Cameron Wright, Derek Calder, John Reid, Iain Scott, Sandy Herd, Mark Turnbull, Ian Rodgerson, Peter Robertson, Rita Storie.
SECOND ROW – Christine Lyon, Margaret Horne, Alison Seeley, Pat Lyle, Frances Robson, Deborah Lyons, Maureen Slorance, Jane Headspeath, Dorothy Meechan, Rosemarie Watt.
FRONT ROW – Janette McGregor, Anne Clark, Margaret White, Anne McCredie, Lesley Stormont, Kathryn Wilson, Norma Harkness, Shelagh Renwick, Pat Esslemont.

Over the last twenty five years the sheer ability and talent displayed by most of the principal role holders has been stunning. From his first appearance as Rolf Gruber, the Nazi cadet, in *The Sound Of Music* (1984), Elliot Goldie, with the full exuberance of youth, romped through a decade of principal parts before gaining a place at London`s Guildhall School of Music to study singing and opera. The part which established him in the Society was that of Arthur Kipps in *Half A Sixpence* (1987) but his portrayal of Tony in *West Side Story* (1991) convinced many that he would be going further afield. HAOS arguably gave him the grounding and platform with which to launch his chosen career.

Anything Goes 1992

Margaret White (Bonnie) lets rip. Norma Harkness and Alison Seeley are in the background.

He was not the only Society member to have taken up singing professionally. Local builder`s son, John McHugh[42] (Cable in *South Pacific* – 1975) also took professional training and graced the London stage with the New D`Oyly Carte Opera Company and the Sadler`s Wells Company (English National Opera). He also sang with Opera de Monte Carlo. Reference has already been made to the singing career of James Dalgleish (*HMS Pinafore* – 1920, *Patience* – 1921) a.k.a. Allan Ramsay. On the purely stage side, Billy Byers,[43] who took minor principal roles with HAOS (1970-1973), went on to a career in stage management, being involved in London productions such as Agatha Christie`s *The Mousetrap*, and some of the recent younger members of the Society, largely owing to Jean Wintrope`s influence, have gone on to study drama and stagecraft.

---

[42] John McHugh today performs under the name of John Hughes in order to satisfy a condition imposed by Equity, the British actors` union.
[43] Billy Byers is the manager of London`s Garrick Theatre.

The Boyfriend 1994

(l-r) BACK – Pat Brady, Linda Sharkey, Alison Seeley, Margaret Horne, Maureen Slorance.
FRONT – Cameron Wright, Sandy Herd, Steve Treacy, Iain Scott

Brigadoon 1995

(l-r) BACK – Brian Ramones, Roger Storie, Cameron Wright, Graeme Johnstone, Rob Goldie, Iain Scott.
MIDDLE – Margaret Slorance, Marie McSherry, Steve Treacy, Malcolm Crosby, Brian Leslie, Alison Seeley, Margaret Horne.
FRONT – Myra McLeod, Susan Dalgleish, Anne Douglas, Claire Newman, Moira Boyd.

Show Boat 1996   The Company

(l-r) BACK ROW – Bill McCraw, Stuart Gibson, Craig McCredie, Des Devine, Cameron Wright, Rob Goldie, Niall Bailey.

THIRD ROW – Alison Seeley, Maureen Slorance, Dorothy Meechan, Derek Calder, Ian Duncan, Eddie Martin, Sandy Herd, Iain Scott, Graeme Johnstone, Pat Lyle, Myra McLeod, Margaret Slorance, Deborah Lyons.

SECOND ROW – Letta Dalgleish, Christine Lyon, Margaret Horne, Gillian Patterson, Jane Headspeath, Susan Dalgleish, Pat Adam, Jan Borthwick, Anne Clark, Moira Boyd.

FRONT ROW – Kim Pender, Kerry Slorance, Claire Newman, Linda Sharkey, Shelagh Renwick, Lesley Fraser, Susan Wright, Anne Douglas, Laureen Kinsella, Marion Waldie, Tanya Slorance.

The final quarter also saw the playing stature of Jim Arbon and Stuart Gibson – Teri talent – rise inexorably. Jim has turned out consistently secure, committed performances over many years. An early triumph was his rendition of Hines in *The Pajama Game* (1981) and, taking smaller parts on the way, he consolidated his reputation as Nicely Nicely Johnson in *Guys And Dolls* (1986) and Harry Chitterlow in *Half A Sixpence* (1987). His Maestro Pisoni in *Song Of Norway* (1988), Big Jule in *Guys And Dolls* (2002) and Shalford in *Half A Sixpence* (2003) were stepping stones to a memorable Billis in *South Pacific* (2006). Stuart Gibson`s career with HAOS followed a similar trajectory, beginning as a minor principal (Pearce) in *Half A Sixpence* (1987), and playing alongside Arbon and Goldie in a show replete with cameo roles taken by Brian Leslie, Patricia Lyle, Peter Robertson and Les Sneddon.

Of all the Society`s `character` actresses, none, arguably, has done it better than Christine Lyon. She bestrides the stage with an authority rooted in recitation and elocution; she has a `stage presence` which she has honed in numerous roles over many years to the great advantage of the Opera and the Two Rivers Theatre Company. Her leading roles in *Call Me Madam* (1977) and *The King And I* (1979) have been supplemented by characterisations like Parthy Ann in *Show Boat* (1996), Mrs. Worthington Worthington in *Me And My Girl* (1997), Mrs. Walsingham in *Half A Sixpence* (2003), Yente, the Matchmaker, in *Fiddler On The Roof* (2005) and the very demanding role of Fraulein Schneider in *Cabaret* (1999). The list goes on, but in addition to her well-crafted stage work, equally valued by the Society has been her contribution as its Treasurer for over twenty years – an enormous responsibility which she has shouldered with conspicuous acumen.

The `nineties and early `noughties` saw HAOS simply awash with people of real stage and singing ability. If Jean Wintrope was indeed the Society`s finest producer, she would certainly have had to travel much further afield to be able to draw on such a reservoir of amateur talent. In addition to the well-respected Stories, Lyons, Lyon, Arbon, Dalgleish, Herd, Gibson, Leslie, Sneddon, Seeley and Robertson, a wave of new incoming talent now flooded into the Society in the persons of Hazel Devlin, Jane Headspeath, Derek Calder, Jan Borthwick, Graeme Johnstone (all from Galashiels) together with recent settlers in Hawick – Dorothy Meechan, Bill McCraw, Mike and Sasha Cound.

For most of the `nineties, Jane Headspeath, Dorothy Meechan, Stuart Gibson and the urbane Des Devine were on a roll – highly versatile people, ripe for moulding by Jean Wintrope. Jane`s roles as Maria (*West Side Story* – 1991), Polly Brown (*The Boyfriend* – 1994), Magnolia (*Show Boat* – 1996) and Sally Brown (*Me And My Girl* – 1997) bespeak an enviable ability and versatility. Similar was Dorothy Meechan`s contribution. A versatile actress, singer and dancer, she was much lauded for her portrayals of Anita (*West Side Story* – 1991), Ado Annie (*Oklahoma* – 1998) and Miss. Adelaide (*Guys And Dolls* – 2002). She was also the Society`s Secretary 1991-1999.

Show Boat 1996

Captain Andy (Bill McCraw) tells an improbable story with affecting action

Hello Dolly! 1999

Marie McSherry as Dolly Gallacher Levi
with (left, back to front) Bill McCraw,
Steve Brown, Jonathan More, Des Devine,
Craig McCredie and (right, back to front)
Jonathan Ellis, John Fowler, Stuart Gibson
and Derek Calder.

Des Devine made his mark as Billy Crocker in *Anything Goes* (1992), Tommy Albright in *Brigadoon* (1995) and Ravenal in *Show Boat* (1996). A suave, gifted player, he was the perfect stage partner for various leading ladies, his portrayal of Sky Masterson in *Guys And Dolls* (2002) being particularly representative of his stagecraft. But he had other character types in his portfolio – Jigger, for example, in *Carousel* (2004).

Sadly, by 2005, all of these people (Headspeath, Meechan, Gibson and Devine) together with Mike and Sacha Cound (who had, as husband and wife, played the leading roles in *The King And I* – 2001) had left the Society and Hawick.

And so the renewal process has to be continually ongoing. Margaret White, Marie McSherry and Frank Barker, all of whom joined the Society for season 1990-91, made conspicuous contributions to its productions. Marie will long be remembered as Dolly Levi, the eponymous heroine of the 1999 show and Bloody Mary in *South Pacific* (2006). Similarly, Frank Barker's Ali Hakim (*Oklahoma* – 1998), Henry Miller (*Calamity Jane* -2000) and Nathan Detroit (*Guys And Dolls* – 2002) may be taken as representative of a stage career playing colourful characters. Margaret White`s stay in Hawick was fairly short. Her talent wasn`t, as those who recall her as Anybody`s in *West Side Story* (1991), Bonnie in *Anything Goes* (1992) and Esther in *Meet Me In St. Louis* (1993) will attest.

With the advent of the new millennium, it seemed as if there would be no halt to the stream of able people wishing to join the Society. And they kept coming – Steve Brown, the Counds, Lyndsey McCredie, Karen Whinham and Frances Robson (now Goldie) to name the more prominent. But in addition to them were the fruits of earlier investment, for example, the people who had been `children` in the shows of the `eighties and `nineties. Of the six children in *Song Of Norway* (1988), four were adult members during the first decade of the new century – Craig McCredie, Lyndsey McCredie, Iain Scott and Tanya Slorance. Three were offspring of former playing members. `Children` from even earlier productions, now adult members, were Leah Graham and Kerry Cumming (daughters of Maureen Slorance), Shelagh Duncan (daughter of John and Audrey Kinghorn) and Lesley Fraser (granddaughter of Ronnie Stormont). The family tradition of HAOS was alive and well, the McCredies being the children of Dance Mistress Anne Anderson (Barker).

A further development which was of benefit to HAOS in the new millennium was the formation of the Two Rivers Theatre Company in 2000 by Jean Wintrope. This re-introduced cross-fertilisation between the Opera and a musico-dramatic and straight drama group – something which had faded in Hawick in the late `sixties and early `seventies with the demise of Hawick Theatre Group. Besides straight drama, Two Rivers allowed for the smaller scale musical or play with incidental music which the larger HAOS would not normally produce. Presentations such as *Annie* and *Oliver* provided scope for children and youth who received an `apprenticeship` on the job with adults, several of whom were already in the Operatic Society. Some of the Two Rivers` adult members were drawn to the Opera – Ian Brotherston, for example, and Karen Whinham who took the leading female role in *South Pacific* (2006) – and vice versa. Karen also had principal roles in *Fiddler On The Roof* (2005), *Carousel* (2004) and *Anything Goes* (2007).

The Society and the National Operatic and Dramatic Association (NODA)

Season 1999-2000 saw the centenary of the National Operatic and Dramatic Association to which, for the greater part of its existence, the Society has been affiliated. This body, often referred to by the acronym NODA, was set up in 1899. It advises societies on all manner of subjects relating to the production of operas, stage musicals and drama. This includes information on release and availability of shows, costumes, scenery, professional services, etcetera – most of which is disseminated to participating societies through the Association`s regular magazine publications, conferences and a nationwide network of representatives operating on a geographical basis. In October, 1999, Hawick Amateur Operatic Society presented the musical *Cabaret* in celebration of the Association`s one hundred years of service – a presentation which demonstrated Derek Calder`s theatrical versatility.

Cabaret (the show) – Autumn, 1999

Produced by Brian McGlasson for the centenary celebrations of the National Operatic and Dramatic Association (NODA) to which Hawick Amateur Operatic Society has been affiliated for most of its existence.

Above – (l-r) BACK – Lynne Hinton, Bill McCraw, Steve Brown, Deboral Lyons, Anne Clark, Mike Cound, Craig Neilson, William Anderson. MIDDLE – Susan Paterson, Iain Scott, Alison Seeley, Christine Lyon, Margaret Horne, Laura Blacklock.
FRONT – Shelagh Renwick, Linda Ness, Heather Paterson, Rhona Scott, Norma Harkness.

Right – Cabaret Girls – 1999
(l-r) BACK – Linda Ness, Anne Clark.
FRONT – Norma Harkness, Deborah Lyons, Shelagh Renwick.

The millennium got off to a dazzling start with a youthful, first-time, glittering performance by Lyndsey McCredie as *Calamity Jane* (2000). Generational overlap was well in evidence in this show with a principals` listing which included Frank Barker, Deborah Lyons, Stuart Gibson, Des Devine and George Storie (forty six years after his HAOS debut). Lyndsey`s brother, Craig McCredie, son of choreographer Anne Anderson, took the lead as Kipps in *Half A Sixpence* (2003), playing to Sasha Cound`s Ann Pornick. Ever an ideal show for `bringing on` aspiring principals with its plethora of good `cameo` parts, it advanced the stagecraft of Rob Goldie, Iain Scott, Lesley Fraser (Stormont),

National Operatic and Dramatic Association (NODA) Conference, Peebles Hydro – 1989   Opera Men
(l-r) Steve Treacy, Brian Leslie, Elliot Goldie, Neil Comely, Stuart Gibson. Craig McCredie in front.

her sister Leanne and her cousin Gillian Patterson (granddaughters of Ronnie Stormont, who had joined HAOS in 1937). Keeping with the theme of family connection, in this show were also Shelagh Renwick (now Duncan) and her son Scott Renwick, daughter and grandson, respectively, of former President of the Society John Kinghorn (1962) and his wife Audrey (Lyon – one of the fresh intake in 1948). Shelagh has also managed to take supporting parts in addition to her work for the Society as Secretary (2002-2010). She is presently the Society`s Vice-President.

Iain Scott merits special mention because since his early experience as a child actor in *Song Of Norway* (1988) he has been one of the most loyal members of the Society, developing his vocal skills and the quality of his stagecraft. 2004 saw him as Enoch Snow in *Carousel*, 2005 as the student Perchik in *Fiddler On The Roof* and, in 2008, he showed his worth as Tommy Albright in *Brigadoon*. If HAOS could be assured of Iain Scott`s level of commitment from all its members, its bi-centenary would be a foregone conclusion. He has always been in it for the long haul and supports all its activities – a `true trouper` would be an apt description of him.

The first nine years of the new millennium, 2000-2008, were characterised by vintage shows, including three Rodgers and Hammerstein classics and *Anything Goes* by Cole Porter. They were years which saw the ascendancy of Steve Brown as an HAOS stalwart. He was also involved with the Two Rivers Theatre Company and his stage career derived great benefit from this dual membership. He wasn`t alone, of course; Marie McSherry, Bill McCraw, Jan Borthwick, Karen Whinham, Stuart Gibson, Jim Arbon, Iain Scott, Peter Robertson, Ian Brotherston, Alison Seeley, Shelagh Duncan and Christine Lyon were principals in the same boat – happily. The common factor in their development, of course, was Jean Wintrope and, to some extent, Derek Calder who, in a number of Two Rivers productions, acted as Musical Director. Steve Brown took leading roles in six of the shows over these nine years, Wild Bill Hickock (*Calamity Jane*), Tevye (*Fiddler On The Roof*), Billy Bigelow (*Carousel*) and Emile de Becque (*South Pacific*) defining his place in the annals of HAOS. Out for 2007 and 2008 owing to work commitments, he was back at the top again for 2009 as the Sheriff in *The Best Little Whorehouse In Texas*.

Deborah Lyons endorsed a long list of leading successes with her Julie Jordan (*Carousel* – 2004), Reno (*Anything Goes* – 2007) and the formidable part of Mona, the brothel owner, in *The Best Little Whorehouse In Texas* (2009). She has been a consistently secure performer at the top for over thirty years, leading in no less than eighteen shows during that time. She is undaunted by complex music and has rarely given a weak account of herself. Her Sarah in *Guys And Dolls* (1986), Sally Bowles in *Cabaret* (1999) and Reno in *Anything Goes*, already mentioned, have defined her contribution to HAOS and she is popular with Hawick audiences. As a performer, her worthiness to occupy the President`s chair cannot be denied and this has fallen to her for the Society`s centenary.

The centenary is a reminder that Hawick Amateur Operatic Society has reached this stage because it has weathered its crises and succeeded in the process of renewal and regeneration. This is still going on as recent performances by Lesley Fraser, Janie Mallin, Louise Szoneberg, Clare Oliver, Tony Randall, Paul Lockie, Steve Law, Caroline Wilkinson, Liam Caswell, Mandy Rayner and Billy Rooney have amply demonstrated. Lesley`s Meg Brockie in *Brigadoon* (2008) was a revelation as was Caroline`s Jewel in *The Best Little Whorehouse In Texas* (2009) and similar claims could made for Liam, Mandy, Clare and Billy in *Copacabana* (2010). In fact, the shock of `new discovery` Billy Rooney as Sam Silver in that show almost upstaged the two highly talented leads, Mandy and Liam, both of whom had worked their way through a few previous shows. In amateur operatics, expect the unexpected!

Me And My Girl 1997 *Doing the Lambeth Walk*
(l-r) Mike Cound, Jane Headspeath, Craig McCredie, Marie McSherry, Steve Treacy and Deborah Lyons.

Oklahoma 1998
Stuart Gibson (Curly), Jan Borthwick (Laurey) and Steve Treacy (Jud Fry)

Oklahoma 1998

(l-r) Dorothy Meechan, Steve Brown, Tanya Slorance, Craig McCredie, Maureen Slorance, Susan Wright, Des Devine.
BACK RIGHT – Cameron Wright, Rita Storie, Derek Calder, Shelagh Renwick.

Dorothy Meechan (Ado Annie) with Derek Calder (Will Parker)

Hello Dolly! 1999

(l-r) BACK – Christine Lyon, Shelagh Renwick, Helen Boles, Heather Paterson, Dorothy Meechan, Margaret Slorance, Jan Borthwick, Moira Boyd, Alison Seeley. MIDDLE – Rhona Scott, Margaret Horne, Susan Paterson, Lynne Hinton. FRONT – Laura Blacklock, Gillian Patterson, Julie Murray.

Harmonica Garden Waiters and Waitresses
(l-r) BACK – Bill McCraw, Jonathan More, Derek Calder, Jonathan Ellis, John Fowler, Craig McCredie, Stuart Gibson. FRONT – Des Devine, Lesley Fraser, Tanya Slorance, Maureen Slorance, Anne Clark, Steve Brown.

Calamity Jane 2000

Left – Siblings – Craig and Lyndsey McCredie.

Lyndsey was the eponymous heroine and this was her adult debut (she is one of the children in the earlier *Song Of Norway* picture).

Below – The `Golden Garter` Girls

(l-r) BACK – Lesley Fraser, Anne Clark, Dorothy Meechan, Gillian Patterson, Tanya Slorance, Kerry Cumming.
FRONT – Julie Murray, Leanne Stormont.

The King And I 2001

Above – Death of the King

The attendants are (l-r) Harry Lightfoot Jnr., Steve Brown, Rob Goldie and Des Devine.

Right – The first husband and wife leads since George and Rita Storie in 1968 (*Bitter Sweet*).

Mike and Sasha Cound as the King and Anna Leonowens.

Guys And Dolls 2002

Left – Dorothy Goldie (Miss. Adelaide) and Sasha Cound (Sarah) share the misery of trying to land a husband.

Below – Crapshooters – Derek Calder (Nicely-Nicely Johnson) and Frank Barker (Nathan Detroit).

Left – Miss. Adelaide (Dorothy Goldie) and the `Hot Box` nightclub girls – (l-r) BACK – Anne Clark, Lesley Fraser, Leanne Stormont, Gillian Patterson, Lyndsey McCredie, Pamela Casson. FRONT – Tanya Slorance, Frances Goldie.

Half A Sixpence 2003

(l-r) BACK – Alison Seeley, Pat Adam, Graham Gordon, Derek Inglis, Shelagh Renwick, Craig McCredie, Sasha Cound, Iain Scott, Scott Renwick, Christine Lyon.
FRONT – Anne Clark, Lesley Fraser, Gillian Patterson, Leanne Stormont, Tanya Slorance, Pamela Casson.

Carousel 2004

(Anti-clockwise from the right)

Carrie Pipperidge (Karen Whinham) with Enoch Snow (Iain Scott)

Louise (Tanya Slorance) with Enoch Snow Jnr, (Stuart Mitchell)

Mr. Bascombe (Frank Barker), Heavenly Friend (Ian Brotherston) and the Starkeeper (Ron Watson)

Billy Bigelow (Steve Brown) with Mrs. Mullin, carousel operator (Alison Seeley)

Billy Bigelow (Steve Brown) with Julie Jordan (Deborah Lyons)

Fiddler On The Roof 2005

Above – (l-r) Niall Campbell (Mendel),
Derek Inglis (Mordeha, innkeeper), Janie Mallin
(villager), Peter Robertson (Avraham, bookseller)

Left – Iain Scott (Perchik the student) with
Leah Graham (Hodel)

South Pacific 2006

Jim Arbon (Luther Billis) with (l-r) Paul Lockie, Craig McCredie, Jonathan Kirk, Stuart Mitchell,
Iain Scott (obscured), Liam Caswell and Jamie Scott.

South Pacific 2006

Nurses (l-r) Morag Bain, Leah Graham, Linda Mason, Gillian Patterson, Pamela Casson, Shelagh Duncan, Anne Clark.

Anything Goes 2007
Craig McCredie (Billy Crocker) with Deborah Lyons (Reno)

Anything Goes 2007
(l-r) Frank Barker (Moonface Martin), Deborah Lyons (Reno), Craig McCredie (Billy Crocker)

There appears to be no shortage of future contenders for principal parts with people like Ashley Wilkinson, Richard Millan, Jo and Emma Law,[44] Ross Aitkin and Rachel Inglis (who has given such good accounts of her abilities with the Two Rivers Theatre Company) already doing more than waiting in the wings.

After the long reign of Jean Wintrope as Producer, the Society secured the services of Brian McGlasson of Innerleithen in 2008. He was already known to the Society, having produced *Cabaret* for them in 1999, and his appointment bids fair for many successes to come. The material is there for him to mould and there are already potential principals awaiting their opportunity. On with the show!

Encore, or Curtains?

There has been much talk of changing the Society`s name, a reason given being that the terms *Operatic* and/or *Society* are inappropriate, off-putting to the young, irrelevant and even archaic. The same could be applied to Hawick Archaeological Society which today does very little digging and could probably be more appropriately termed Hawick Historical Society, or to Hawick Sax-Horn Band which could simply be Hawick Brass Band. Among the reasons why their names have *not* been changed is that they incorporate an implied recognition of, and pride in, their history – in the case of the band, the development of the instruments they play by Adolphe Sax (of saxophone fame) c. 1845 and the fact that the Hawick band was among the first Scottish bands to take on the full complement of such instruments. Accordingly, there is a respect for the history of the band implied in its name, which it does not require audiences or even participants to understand. Only if they are interested need they delve further; they have the choice. Removal of, or supplanting, the name removes this choice unless a subtitle like *formerly Hawick Amateur Operatic Society* is employed. Without such, a different or new society is formed in a similar fashion to the discarding of the name Hawick Amateur Operatic Company in favour of Hawick Amateur Operatic Society. However it is regarded, a change of name, in this case, would be difficult to dissociate psychologically from `the end of an era`. Perhaps the choice for this amazing association of talented, creative people, vibrant humanity at its best, Hawick Amateur Operatic Society, is indeed encore or curtains! Or is it all semantics? Watch this space.

---

[44] Their great great aunt, Mary Boles, had a principal part (O Lia San) in *Viktoria And Her Hussar* 1938.

Chapter IX

OFFSTAGE AND BEHIND THE SCENES

Most perceptive theatre goers are aware that to have the presentation before them on stage, a small army is at work in the background, oiling the wheels, changing the scenery, preparing the `props`, assisting with quick costume change, make-up and generally assisting performers to `get out there` and deliver. Yet surprisingly, or perhaps unsurprisingly, no mention of a stage manager, let alone scene shifters, appears in the Society`s programmes until 1960 (*Rose Marie*) when David Stothart is officially recognised as such, with an assistant stage manager, Mrs. Jan Blackwood, to boot. Indeed, in the first programme after the War, 1948, no ancillary background staff are recognised unless they are paid professionals. Only hired purveyors of costumes, scenery and make-up appear to be worthy of mention although, to be fair, J.E.D.

Murray, as make-up artist, was credited from the very first show in 1911 to his final input in 1935. Yet those who have been involved in such presentations know that someone has to collect and collate costume measurements, for example, and erect and paint scenery and organise properties.

In former days, much of the costume hire arrangements would be supervised by the Secretary with co-opted assistance from a lady and gentleman in the cast. After the Second World War, former players did assist with wardrobe and make-up, Jean Gladstone and her fellow founding member Sarah Armstrong, among them, with assistance from Jenny Townsend and Neil Wintrope. They were only officially recognised from 1953 and only from 1957 was make-up by Andrew H. Wilkinson, David Hobbs and W. S. Scrimgeour (Headmaster of Trinity School) recognised. In her role as wardrobe mistress, many will recall May Matthews (Watters) with affection. She was one of the `characters` of the Opera – another of those gems (and former player) who would do anything for the Society`s well being. A glance at a recent programme will demonstrate just how much things have

What isn`t seen!
Brian Thomson (seated) and Andrew Smith
programme the lighting

changed, and today the Society tries to acknowledge formally *all* who in any way assist in getting the show on the road.

Stothart was followed as stage manager by many stalwarts, among them Dougie Fisher, Eddie Hill, Bill Scott, Keith McCredie, Robert McKean and Robbie Duncan, all assisted by their mates and often by former playing members. Bill Scott and Gordon Smart were very much a team in the early `seventies, often assisted by the likes of Bill Tait and Jim Wallace if they happened not to be playing in a particular year. The new millennium, however, has seen a regular complement of stage crew give their all to the Society – Findlay Adam, Bill Anderson, Dougie Anderson, Tam Inglis and Jim Wallace, to name them.

It is humbling to discover that Brian Thomson is first recorded in respect of stage lighting in 1967 and, along with his apprentice of nearly fourteen years (Andrew Smith), is still doing it. Similar is the service of Bill Abbott, who supervised the sound system for over thirty years before handing over to Colin Blaikie. Pat Adam, though a committed playing member, has been organising costumes since 1985; her colleague, Ann Szoneberg, will alter a costume at the drop of a hat. Margaret Spalding has been involved in make-up for almost twenty years, taking over from Audrey Kinghorn and Frances Carruthers, and Mary Blacklock, following the redoubtable Gwen Shortreed, has been hair stylist since 1990. And then there is Margaret Allan who, until recently, from time immemorial it seems, organised the programme sales. Who can deny the Society has been well served by its ancillary team?

Mary Blacklock, hair stylist, with Shelagh Duncan

Jimmy Anderson prepares lunch for the orchestra (whose members come from all over the Borders) on the day of the Dress Rehearsal

Chapter X

PLUGGING THE GAP

It may surprise, even shock, the reader to learn that the expense of mounting a musical theatre production in Hawick Town Hall for a week is now approaching £20,000 – an escalation which threatens the very existence of the Society. This sum has to be offset by raising income, the main volume of which has to come from the sale of tickets. The problem is as old as the Society itself; keeping the tickets moderately priced, yet balancing the books. The biggest outlay is the cost of hiring the Town Hall, and it seems incredible that what the old Hawick Town Council granted free, gratis and for nothing for one year (1913) is now the subject of a £2,000-£2,500 charge. How perverse and mercenary `local` government has now become; the very institutions that make for good community life are now in real danger of being bled out of existence. To help defray these excessive charges, HAOS must now run various fund-raising activities – concerts, cabarets, coffee mornings, quizzes, race nights and sales – anything, in fact, that may assuage an ever-present financial predicament and headache for the Society`s office-bearers.

Fundraising cabaret in Town Hall – 1989   Opera Ladies

(l-r) Pat Rolland, Maureen Slorance, Myra McLeod, Margaret Horne, Alison Seeley. Dorothy Meechan in front.

The Social Committee

HAOS Social Committee is a major contributor to the reduction of these problems, raising money through the sale of refreshments, wine, etcetera at performance intervals and running raffles and sales. The Committee was instituted on 21st June, 1965, in order to arrange a Gala Night on the Saturday prior to Opera Week in 1966 with the purpose of supplanting the Saturday matinee which could not be held because there was insufficient `blacking out` in the newly refurbished and extended Town Hall. The plan was to neutralise the projected financial loss incurred through not having the matinee. The Committee comprised founder member Mrs. Ina Johnstone, Bailie Mrs. Helen Scott, Mrs. Eileen Smith and Messrs. James Anderson, William Jardine and James Murray, with Adam R. Hogg as convenor. The Gala Night, however, it was reported in the *Hawick Express* (9/3/66) –

> "..failed to come up to crowd expectations, and it is doubtful whether the extra performance, even at £1 per head, including supper served in the newly-opened Lesser Hall, will pay its way......."

An inauspicious start, then, but the Social Committee was here to stay. It was charged with arranging a Bazaar in the Town Hall on Saturday, 9th November, 1968, "the purpose of which is to raise funds to offset the very considerable cost which is anticipated for the Society`s forthcoming production of *My Fair Lady.*" Bailie Mrs. Helen Scott was now convenor and the stallholders included Rita Storie, May Matthews, Maisie Ormiston, Rena Townsend, Brenda Walker, Eleanor Dalgleish, Margaret Logan, Myra McLeod, Norman Graham (newsagent), Jimmy Murray and Jimmy Anderson. And guess what? Forty two years on, Jimmy Anderson is still the mainstay of the Social Committee, and the aims and objects detailed for this Bazaar remain unchanged; simply substitute the present show, or projected show, for *My Fair Lady.*

The present Social Committee, numbering sixteen, are all former players, with the exception of Netta Wallace (Ex-President Jim`s wife), Angie Purvis and her mother Edna (whose other daughter and granddaughter are playing members), Monica Law and Ann Inglis, who also assists with make-up. During Opera Week, the Committee is essentially part of a front-of-house team who, together with `doorpersons` (also former playing members), serve and greet the public. It would be remiss to omit two other front-of-house people, in a literal sense, who serve both public and players, namely, Neil Corbett, who over many years has taken on the mantle of J.E.D. Murray, photographer, and recorded many scenes of happiness, and Etta McKean who, following in the footsteps of Andrew White, John Forrest, Alice Walker, John Walsh and Wilma Waters, has embraced the prompter`s role with consummate professionalism.

Chapter XI

CHOICE OF SHOW

An operatic society's success depends ultimately upon its ability to please audiences and engage their continued interest. The relationship between the society and its audience is complex, involving not only the individual and collective talents of the players but the astuteness of the society in gauging the public mood and balancing it with the stimulation of the players themselves. Universal loyalty is not automatic – unfortunately – from both sides. Irrespective of what the society might wish for from its members, it has been noted previously that, for various reasons, some of its personnel drift in and out of participation (they don't like the show selected, or there is `no part for me`, or `I'm not doing, or wearing, that`). Loyalty can be hard-won and such a scenario is not endemic to Hawick – it occurs in the majority of amateur societies. Equally, audience loyalty cannot be assumed, but has to be

The Best Little Whorehouse In Texas 2009

Clockwise from bottom left (follow up staircase)– Fergus Hyslop, Caroline Wilkinson, Marie McSherry, Paul Lockie, Clare Oliver, Ashley Wilkinson, Iain Scott, Jason Hart, Gillian Patterson, Louise Szoneberg, Richard Millan, Craig McCredie, David Patterson (semi obscured), Jamie Scott, Leanne Turnbull, Alison Seeley, Julie Murray, Natalie Paterson, Steven Law, Laura Randall.

earned. People, asked to pay good money, expect to see `good, wholesome entertainment.` HAOS has not been the first amateur society to get it wrong occasionally, nor will it be the last.

Yet a progressive society must be prepared, occasionally, to take a risk with a relatively unknown show. In any society there are competing interests and diverse agendas, and a glance through the Hawick society`s list of previous productions may prompt questions as to what influences were at work behind a certain choice of show in spite of the long shadow cast by the balance sheet. Was the choice of *Robert And Elizabeth* (1970), for example, affected by the presence in the Society of a very strong representation of Hawick Theatre Group members? Was *The Best Little Whorehouse In Texas* (2009) a cry for greater public attention, or did it arise from a need within the Society `to find something different` – perhaps rather more for the sake of its members than its patrons? Was the accolade of `British Premiere`, trumpeted on the Society`s *Meet me In St. Louis* (1993) programme, worth the candle for a somewhat lack-lustre show?

From the latter, audiences had the pleasure of hearing and recalling two classic numbers in the form of *The Trolley Song* and *Have Yourself A Merry Little Christmas* but who, among the Society`s most ardent devotees, can recall a single melody from *Robert And Elizabeth* or *The Best Little Whorehouse In Texas*, let alone dinosaurs like *The Nautch Girl*, in spite of irreproachable performances in these shows?

It is an obvious truism that, from the point of view of the audience, the most successful shows are those which have a readily comprehensible story line and which contain between three and half a dozen really good, memorable showstoppers. Most of the Gilbert and Sullivan operettas meet such criteria, as do the works of Rodgers and Hammerstein, Sigmund Romberg, Lerner and Loewe and Cole Porter together with isolated shows like *The Arcadians, Oliver, Annie, Guys And Dolls, West Side Story, The Merry Widow, Calamity Jane, Me And My Girl, The Boyfriend, Half A Sixpence, Annie,Get Your Gun, Show Boat, Fiddler On The Roof, Seven Brides For Seven Brothers* and *Cabaret.* (The same criteria hold for `non-amateur-released` contemporary shows like *Les Misérables, Chicago* and *The Phantom Of The Opera*).

Other shows fall into a kind of `hit nor miss` category, and where they do succeed, it is often owing to some special attribute in production or other discipline such as dance. An intrinsically `weak` show may be deemed a success through spectacular means. Gilbert and Sullivan`s *Ruddigore* with its picture gallery of ancestors coming to life is one example of this.

The challenge, then, for HAOS (or any other amateur operatic society) is to continually find a show which has the potential to be truly memorable for both audience and players for the right reasons. For a society such as HAOS, whose deficit on a production currently runs at over £5000, it is a challenge which requires the most earnest consideration. The shows, over the piece, must satisfy the paying public yet simultaneously stimulate the players; the books have ultimately to balance in order to ensure the Society`s survival. Difficult one.

For the record, in its one hundred years, the works most frequently selected by HAOS (thrice each) have been *The Mikado* (1913, 1923, 1934), *The Desert Song* (1935, 1952, 1976), *Oklahoma* (1955, 1967, 1998), *The King And I* (1964, 1979, 2001), and *South Pacific* (1975, 1985, 2006). A similar pattern, albeit with some variation of show, can be observed in the annals of the other Border societies.

Chapter XII

EPILOGUE

The Opera is a complex organisation which has to work as a complete team in order to ensure its survival. The people who work behind the scenes, the coffee makers, programme sellers, photographers, costumiers, make-up artists, sound controllers and lighting technicians are in every way as vital to the finished product as the people on stage, a fact that those who most readily reap the plaudits must now recognise. A duff sound controller, for example, can now ruin a performance in a far more devastating manner than could the rainstorm which buffeted the Town Hall roof during the opening night of *HMS Pinafore* in 1920.

Teamwork, loyalty, service, dedication and perseverance, together with a family and community spirit, are the key elements of a story in which Hawick should take great satisfaction and pride. It is in these principles that the future of HAOS lies.

Nonagenarian Past President
John Walsh and Betty Howarth
review photographs
with Ian Seeley.

Betty, now in her late eighties, is one of
only a handful of members still alive who
joined in 1947 as part of the new intake
after the Second World War.
Also making their Opera debut in 1948
were Jean Whillans (Wintrope) and
Madge Robson (Elliot).

The Society on its Centenary – November, 2010

BACK – B. McGlasson, D. Calder, D. Wolf, C. Blaikie, B. Rooney, R. Goldie, T. Inglis, R. Millan, L. Scott, C. Kyle, F. Hislop, D. Paterson, S. Brown, R. Aitkin, S. Law, J. Arbon, A. Blacklock. THIRD ROW – A. Gordon, A. Inglis, M. Spalding, R. Watson, J. Wilkinson, R. Duncan, A. Clark, M. Boyd, E. Halliday, P. Scott, L. Szoneberg, C. Oliver, M. Tolland, L. Dalgleish, M. Blacklock, J. Anderson, M. Logan, E. Purvis, M. Horne, M. Slorance, A. Ford, N. Wallace. SECOND ROW – A. Gaston, A. Anderson, W. Waters, C. McCredie, P. Adam, F. Barker, S. Duncan, D. Lyons, C. Wilkinson, C. Lyon, A. Seeley, J. Wallace, M. Ormiston, M. Allan, I. McLeod. FRONT – F. Goldie, L. Farmer, G. Patterson, L. Fraser, L. Turnbull, E. Law, J. Mallin, R. Inglis, L. Coburn, N. Paterson, A. Wilkinson. Unable to be present – F. Adam, W. Anderson, E. Armstrong, J. Borthwick, T. Borthwick, P. Casson, N. Corbett, J. Law, M. Law, P. Lockie, M. McSherry, S. Paterson, L. Randall, T. Randall, M. Rayner, L. Renwick, A. Smith, K. Sykes, A. Szoneberg, B. Thomson, M. Van Beek, J. Walsh.

APPENDICES

- List of Shows, Producers, Musical Directors

- Presidents of the Society

- Common-Riding People and the Opera

- First Appearances of Performers

Year	Show	Producer	Musical Director
1911	HMS Pinafore	John S. Brewster, Edinburgh	Robert Rimmer
1912	The Pirates of Penzance	" " "	" "
1913	The Mikado	" " "	" "
1914	Iolanthe	" " "	" "
1915-1919	WAR YEARS AND RE-SETTLEMENT – NO SHOW		
1920	HMS Pinafore	John S. Brewster, Edinburgh	William Campbell
1921	Patience	" " "	" "
1922	The Gondoliers	" " "	" "
1923	The Mikado	" " "	" "
1924	The Yeomen of the Guard	" " "	" "
1925	Iolanthe	" " "	" "
1926	The Nautch Girl	" " "	" "
1926	The Pirates of Penzance	" " "	" "
1927	NO SHOW		
1928	The Gondoliers	" " "	" "
1929	Ruddigore	" " "	" "
1930	A Country Girl	" " "	" "
1931	The Arcadians	" " "	" "
1932	The Damask Rose	" " "	" "
1933	Florodora	Gordon Stamford, London	" "
1934	The Mikado	John S. Brewster, Edinburgh	" "
1935	The Desert Song	Jack Lennox, Edinburgh	" "
1936	Rose Marie	Gordon Stamford, London	" "
1937	The Student Prince	Frances Davis, London	" "
1938	Viktoria And Her Hussar	" " "	" "
1939	The Vagabond King	Frances Davis, London	" "
1940-1947	WAR YEARS AND RE-SETTLEMENT – NO SHOW		
1948	A Country Girl	J. Hebden Foster, Edinburgh	William Campbell
1949	Rio Rita	Jack Lennox, Edinburgh	" "
1950	The New Moon	" " "	" "
1951	The Quaker Girl	" " "	Richard More (W.C.)
1952	The Desert Song	Frances Davis, London	" " (W.C.)
1953	Nina Rosa	" " "	Eric A. Whitehead (W.C.)
1954	Pink Champagne	" " "	" " (W.C.)
1955	Oklahoma	" " "	" " (E.D.)
1956	Balalaika	" " "	" " (E.D.)
1957	Love From Judy	" " "	" " (E.D.)
1958	White Horse Inn	Claud Worth, Edinburgh	" " (N.W.)
1959	Annie Get Your Gun	Barbara Ross	" " (N.W.)
1960	Rose Marie	Edward Horton, Edinburgh	" " (N.W.)
1961	Summer Song	" " "	" " (W.D.E.)
1962	The Dancing Years	Thomas I. McIntyre, Haddington	" " (W.D.E.)
1963	Wild Grows The Heather	Edward Horton, Edinburgh	" " (W.D.E.)
1964	The King And I	" " "	David Young
1965	The Merry Widow	" " "	" "
1966	Bitter Sweet	" " "	" "
1967	Oklahoma	Donald Norris, Workington	" "
1968	Wild Violets	Tom Fidelo, Edinburgh	David Griffiths

Year	Show	Producer	Musical Director
1969	My Fair Lady	Phyllis Ward, Edinburgh	David Griffiths
1970	Robert And Elizabeth	Phyllis Ward, Edinburgh	Mary D. Rowell
1971	The Sound Of Music	" " "	" "
1972	Show Boat	" " "	" "
1973	Carousel	Thomas McIntyre, Haddington	" "
1974	White Horse Inn	Elizabeth Seton, Edinburgh	" "
1975	South Pacific	Elizabeth Seton, Edinburgh	Mary D. Rowell
1976	The Desert Song	" " "	David Young
1977	Call Me Madam	" " "	" "
1978	Bless The Bride	Jean M. Wintrope, Hawick	Betty Scott
1979	The King And I	" " "	Basil Deane
1980	NO SHOW		
1981	The Pajama Game	Kedzie Penfield/ Stephen Fox	Stephen Fox
1982	Flower Drum Song	Jean M. Wintrope, Hawick	Betty Scott
1983	Balalaika	" " "	Susan Booth
1984	The Sound Of Music	Christine Lyon, Hawick	Betty Scott
1985	South Pacific	" " "	Edward A. Ferguson
1986	Guys And Dolls	Bill Harvey, Innerleithen	" "
1987	Half A Sixpence	" " "	Ian W. Seeley
1988	Song Of Norway	" " "	" "
1989	Kiss Me, Kate	" " "	David Young
1990	Seven Brides For Seven Brothers	Jean M. Wintrope, Hawick	Mary D. Rowell
1991	West Side Story	" " "	" "
1992	Anything Goes	" " "	Chris Achenbach
1993	Meet Me In St. Louis	" " "	" "
1994	The Boyfriend	" " "	" "
1995	Brigadoon	" " "	Robert Howden (D.C.)
1996	Show Boat	" " "	Ian W. Seeley
1997	Me And My Girl	" " "	Chris Achenbach
1998	Oklahoma	" " "	Colin Fox
1999	Hello, Dolly!	Jean M. Wintrope, Hawick	James Letham
1999	Cabaret	Brian McGlasson, Innerleithen	" "
2000	Calamity Jane	Jean M. Wintrope, Hawick	" "
2001	The King And I	" " "	Chris Achenbach (D.M.)
2002	Guys And Dolls	" " "	James Letham
2003	Half A Sixpence	" " "	Derek Calder
2004	Carousel	" " "	" "
2005	Fiddler On The Roof	" " "	" "
2006	South Pacific	" " "	" "
2007	Anything Goes	" " "	" "
2008	Brigadoon	" " "	" "
2009	The Best Little Whorehouse In Texas	Brian McGlasson, Innerleithen	" "
2010	Copacabana	" " "	" "
2011	Beauty And The Beast	" " "	" "

CHORUS MASTERS D.C. – Derek Calder; W.C. – William Campbell; E.D. – Eleanor Dalgleish; W.D.E. – William Deans Ellis; D.M. – David MacKay; N.W. – Nan Whillans

PRODUCERS FOR HAWICK AMATEUR OPERATIC SOCIETY

Hawick Amateur Operatic Society has worked under the direction of eighteen different producers. Originally, such were known as `dramatic coaches`, but every player knows what they do and how they operate and, because their role is much more `interpretive` of the librettists`s scripts, in contrast to the MD`s more `recreative` role, their shorter annual relationship with the company is usually much more intense and `personality` affected. It would be true to say that Hawick has experienced some remarkable `personalities` in the sphere of theatrical production. Most have been highly competent, each with his or her own idio -syncratic method of reaching the final goal; some, like Frances Davis, `Teddy` Horton and Jean M. Wintrope have been outstanding in the long history of the Society.

1.   John S. Brewster
2.   Gordon Stamford
3.   Jack Lennox
4.   Frances Davis
5.   J. Hebden Foster
6.   Claud Worth
7.   Barbara Ross
8.   Edward Horton
9.   Thomas I. McIntyre
10. Donald Norris
11. Tom Fidelo
12. Phyllis Ward
13. Elizabeth Seton
14. Jean M. Wintrope
15. Kedzie Penfield
16. Christine Lyon
17. Bill Harvey
18. Brian McGlasson

MUSICAL DIRECTORS OF HAWICK AMATEUR OPERATIC SOCIETY

Being musical director of an operatic society requires enormous dedication, tact and limitless patience. As the name implies, the presentation of a musical demands that before an thing can be staged, the music must be taught and rehearsed until it becomes second nature to the players. The pressure on the MD begins at the first practice of the season and remains until the final curtain falls on the show because, unlike the producer, the MD is an actual performer in the final product – visibly accountable for what emanates from the stage and from the band of instrumentalists which he has had to engage and assemble on behalf of the society. The latter, in itself, can be an onerous responsibility where particular musicians are in short supply. From its earliest days, HAOS has required to hire musicians from all over the Borders and, frequently, from further afield. The Society has had seventeen musical directors in its century of existence.

1. Robert Rimmer
2. William Campbell
3. Richard More
4. Eric A. Whitehead
5. David Young
6. David Griffiths
7. Mary D. Rowell
8. Betty Scott
9. Basil Deane
10. Stephen Fox
11. Susan M. Booth
12. Edward A. Ferguson
13. Ian W. Seeley
14. Chris Achenbach
15. James Letham
16. Colin Fox
17. Derek Calder

PRESIDENTS OF HAOS

1910	John Hume *
1911	William E. Wilson
1912-28	Robert Wilson
1929-50	John Campbell
1951-52	Robert Baxter
1953-55	David O. Stothart
1956-58	John Forrest
1959-61	Ian MacDonald
1962	John Kinghorn
1963-64	John Walsh
1965-68	Ella Haig
1969	Adam R. Hogg**
1970-75	James W. Murray
1976-77	J. Norman Graham
1978-79	ames W. Murray
1980	NO PRODUCTION
1981-82	Edward Martin
1983	Wilma Waters
1984-86	James Wallace
1987-88	John Walsh
1989	Gwen Shortreed
1990-95	Brian Leslie
1996-97	Jane Headspeath
1998-99	Patricia Adam
2000-01	Deborah Lyons
2002-04	Frank Barker
2005-06	Craig McCredie
2007-10	Susan Paterson
2011-	Deborah Lyons

*   John Hume resigned after a few weeks and William E. Wilson stood in.

**   Adam R. Hogg died in office 30/11/69.

Dates refer to the years of the shows during which the person was President e.g. Robert Wilson was elected President at the AGM of 1911, John Campbell similarly in 1928 etc.

COMMON-RIDING PEOPLE AND THE OPERA

One of the most notable features of Hawick is the cross-association in membership of societies and clubs. These assist in binding a close community network in which the Opera has played its part. Over the past century, Opera principals have sung at Common-Riding functions like the Colour Bussing Ceremony, but some members have had a deeper interest as principals and officials in Hawick's historic festival.

Cornets –	J.E.D. Murray (1890)	Opera make-up artist 1911-1935 (also did make-up for HAOC 1898-99)
	James Sutherland (1901)	Tenor lead in *HMS Pinafore* (1911)
	Derek Inglis (1978)	Parts in *Guys And Dolls* (2002), *Half A Sixpence* (2003), *Fiddler On The Roof* (2005), Chorus 2004
Cornets` Lasses –	Henrietta (Etta) Guy (1913) (Cornet R. Elder)	Hebe in *HMS Pinafore* (1911)
	Peggy (Margaret) Davidson (1919) (Cornet Tom Winning)	Josephine in *HMS Pinafore* (1920)
	Maureen Bruce (Simpson)(1954) (Cornet Bruce Mactaggart)	Choreographer 1962-1964
	Evelyn Armstrong (1959) (Cornet Norman Murray)	Dancer 1956
	Joyce Robson (1971) (Cornet Drew Martin)	Chorus 1972-1973
	Maureen Lunn (1978) (Cornet Derek Inglis)	Dancer & minor part in *White Horse Inn* (1974)
	Gillian Patterson (1997) (Cornet Stuart Irvine)	Chorus, dancer, minor parts 1996 –
Acting Fathers –	J.E.D. Murray (1901, 1905, 1912, 1925 – Cornets Sutherland, W.E. Kyle, Bonsor, G.D. Scott)	Make-up – as before
	Robert Baxter (1929)[44] (Cornet R.A.V. Grieve)	Chorus & principal parts 1923-1936 President of HAOS 1951-1956
	John Miller Ballantyne (1935)[45] (Cornet W. Brydon)	Founder member, chorus 1911-1914 Orchestra – drums 1948-1951
	Kenneth McCartney (2000)[46] (Cornet Bruce Richardson)	Children`s chorus, *The King And I* (1964)
Acting Mother –	Mary Storie (Murray) (1951) (Cornet George Aitken)	Chorus 1931 – mother of George and Sybil Storie
Official Song Singers –	Harry Storrie (1948-1972)	Chorus & small parts 1936-1939
	Robert (Bert) Armstrong (1973-1984)	Chorus & small parts 1951-1955
	Michael Aitken (2000 –	Chorus & small parts 1978, 1979, 2002

---

[44] Robert Baxter was President of Hawick Callants` Club 1948
[45] John Ballantyne was President of Hawick Rugby Club, 1955-57
[46] Kenneth W. McCartney was Honorary Provost of Hawick, 2005-2007

FIRST APPEARANCES OF PERFORMERS

* Denotes orchestra or band on stage; © denotes Conductor

1911

AITKEN, Adam
ANDERSON, A
ANDERSON, A*
ANDERSON, John
ARMSTRONG, Sarah
BALL, J.C.*
BALLANTYNE, John M.
BALLANTYNE, Walter*
BEATTIE, A.*
BISHER, H.P.
CAMPBELL, J.*
CAMPBELL, John
CAMPBELL, William*
CHARTERS, Ellen
DOUGLAS, G.B.
ELLIOT, John*
GAYLOR, William P.
GLADSTONE, Jean
GLADSTONE, Lizzie
GLENDINNING, J.
GUY, Etta
HARDIE, William P.
HENDERSON, Bessie
HOWARTH, James
HUNTER, E.D.*
INGLES, James
IMRIE, John s.*
KYLE, George A.
LUCK, James D.
McBEAN, D.S.
McVITTIE, M.*
MILLER, Beatrice
MILLER, Jessie
MILLIGAN, Jean
MOYES, W.*
MURRAY, Bella
RAE, J.
RIDDLE, Walter*
RIMMER, Edith
RIMMER, Robert©
SCOTT, B.*
SCOTT, Matthew
SCOTT, M.O.
SCOTT, Molly
SCOTT, William
STEWART, Agnes
SUTHERLAND, James

SWINTON, John D.*
TAIT, Ada
TAIT, Annie
TAYLOR, Beaumont*
TAYLOR, Lizzie
TURNBULL, Ina
TURNBULL, Joe
TURNBULL, Walter
WHITE, Mary
WILLIAMSON, Robert
WILSON, James,
WILSON, Robert
YOUNG, John H.

1912

ARMSTRONG, Mary
CLARK, Jessie
CLARK, Tina
COOPER, Mrs.
GRAY, Frank
HAIG, Bella
IRVINE, Lizzie
LEITHEAD, Adam
MURRAY, Jessie E.
ROGER, John
TODD, Frank W.
TURNBULL, Maxwell
TURNBULL, William D.
WILSON, Annie M.

1913

BELL, Andrew
CLARK, Lizzie
ELLIOT, Mrs. G.
GRAY, Bella
KIRSOPP, John
LAIDLAW, William
SCOTT, Lizzie
TELFER, John
THOMSON, Bella
TURNBULL, Thomas
WALLACE, James
WHEELANS, Stanley
WILSON, Robert Carlyle

1914

BEST, J.
DRYDEN, N
FAIRBAIRN, H.
HOULISTON, David
McCALLUM, Madge
McINTYRE, M.
MITCHELL, Alexander*
TAIT, W.
TOWNSEND, Jenny

1920

AITKEN, George
ALLAN, Mrs.
BALLANTYNE, Mary
BEATTIE, Jessie
BEVERIDGE, Andrew*
BROWN, Lilly
CAIRNS, Agnes
CLARKE, John
DALGLEISH, James
DAVIDSON, Eustace*
ELLIOT, Archibald*
ELLIOT, Jean
GIBSON, Mrs.
HAY, John*
HELM, John
HENDERSON, Ada
HUGGAN, William
HUNTER, Peggy
McKIE, Florence
MILLAR, Annie
MILLAR, Bella
MOFFAT, Robert*
PATERSON, Bella
PRINGLE, C.A.
ROBSON, John
RODGER, Jessie
RILEY, Mrs.
SCOTT, John*
SHORTREED, Thomas E.
SMITH, Annie
SMITH, John E.
SNOWIE, Agnes
STOTHART, David O.
TAIT, Ella
WHILLANS, William J.
WILSON, Agnes

1921

COCHRANE, Miss.*
COCHRANE, Miss. N.*
COCKBURN, Jean
CORBETT, Walter
CROZIER, Miss. B.*
CURRIE, James*
DALGLEISH, George
DARLING, Robert
HENDERSON, Norman C.
JOHNSTON, Miss. M.*
JOHNSTONE, John
LILLICO, Richard
NELSON, Agnes
PARK, John
RUTHERFORD, W.
SCOTT, David C.
SCOTT, Robert
SHEARMAN, Thomas A.
TAIT, James
WARWICK, Greta

1922

BEERS, Bernard*
BONSOR, John O.
CROZIER, Theodore*
DOUGLAS, Doris
DOUGLAS, Walter
GRAY, Mary
GREIG, T.C.*
HILL, John
JOHNSTONE, Marie
LEES, W.D.H.
PRINGLE, Jean
TAYLOR, Mary
THOMSON, Effie
TURNBULL, Donald
WATT, Mark*

1923

BAXTER, Robert
CLIFFORD, Mr.*
CRAE, James
KEDDIE, Walter*
RORRISON, Walter*
SCOTT, Thomas Cowan
WOODS, David

1924

BURKE, Albert E.*
DOBSON, Reginald*
DUNLOP, Thomas
FOX, Peter
HALLIDAY, R.*
HOLT, H.*
HUNTER, John
JOHNSON, Cyril
ROBERTSON, William*
ROBSON, Thomas
TELFER, Gilbert*

1925

BAND, H.*
BRASH, Emily
DAVIDSON, Archibald
GRANT, R.B.
LAIDLAW, Mary
LITTLE, Robert
MIDDLETON, J.W.*
REID, Archibald*
RICHARDS, J.*
WALDIE, Robert
YOUNG, Agnes

1926 (A)

BROWN, R.*
GRAY, F.*
McHUGH, J.
PROUD, H.*
STREETS, Robert*
TURNBULL, Madge

1926 (B)

CUMMING, Margaret (Peggy)
DODDS, J.
FARRIES, Nainie
HODSON, Mr.*
JEFFREY, G.*
LINN, John*
McCARTNEY, M.
RUTHERFORD, W.
TAYLOR, E.
WELCH, John J.

1927

NO SHOW

1928

AITHIE, William*
ARMSTRONG, John*
BARCLAY, Frank*
BRIDICOMBE, W.
CLARK, Maimie B.
EDMONSON, J. Murray*
FORSYTH, David*
HESSEY, John*
LAMB, Cathie
LAMB, M.
MILLER, T. C.*
PICKTHALL, William
WATSON, J.
WILSON, Betty

1929

ANGUS, R.
BOYD, J.*
DAVIDSON, Lena
DAVIDSON, T.*
GARRET, George*
HELM, Thomas jnr.*
HOBKIRK, J.
McKIE, Margaret D.
MORE, Richard*
PEDEN, Walter
TURNBULL, Thomas

1930

ANGUS, J.
BARRIE, Eileen
BEATTIE, Ella
CAMPBELL, Robert
DOUGLAS, Christina
ELDER, Peggy
FAIRBAIRN, Isa
FISHER, Miss. E.
GLADSTONE, Madge
GRAHAM, James
HALL, George
JARDINE, James
McDONALD, D.
MURDOCH, Christina
ROBSON, D.

RODDAN, Robert
SCOTT, Miss. B.
SCOTT, Miss. I.
THOMSON, Margaret
TURNBULL, Alice
TURNBULL, Charles
TURNBULL, Prudence
WILKINSON, Andrew H.
WINTROPE, Ina

1931

BLAKE, Walter
EMERY, Leslie
GRAHAM, D.
HEPBURN, Jessie
HUNTER, Miss. P.
LITTLE, Hamilton B.
MARSCHNER, Louie
MURRAY, Mary
WILSON, Jack*

1932

BEGBIE, J.*
CARRUTHERS, Elsie
CARRUTHERS, Ian
DUNCAN, J.
GRAHAM, R.*
HUGGAN, John
YOUNG, Miss. B.

1933

BEVERIDGE, Eleanor
ELDER, Walter
IRVINE, Sidney (Syd)
KERR, Miss. J.
LANGDALE, Reginald
McCALLUM, Mrs. Hugh
PYM, Ernest
ROBSON, Walter
SCOTT, John

1934

BARRIE, May
BURRELL, Andrew*
CAIRNS, E.
COZIER, F.
DIXON, Mr.*
FORREST, John

HOGG, Mrs. A.B.
McKENNIE, E.
OLIVER, Adam
PATERSON, Maxwell C.
STEWART, Jack
THOMSON, S.
WATTERS, May
WHILLANS, James A.W.
WHITELAW, Mrs.
WOOD, G.

1935

ARMSTRONG, D.
BARCLAY, Miss. B.*
BROWN, John W.*
CLEGG, Charles*
FISHER, George
GALLAGHER, Peter*
HOGG, Adam
KYLE, Elliot O.
ROMANIS, Archie
WALLACE, W.

1936

AITKEN, Mary
AITKEN, Nancy
ARMSTRONG, J.
CLAPPERTON, R.*
DOUGLAS, Jean
HUGGAN, Betty
IRVINE, M.
JAMES, Constance*
JOHNSTONE, May
KENNEDY, J.
MICHIE, P.
MURRAY, G.
OLIVER, Peggy
ROBSON, M.
ROBSON, Nellie
SCOON, Agnes
SCOON, Thomas*
STEVENSON, Nancy
STORRIE, Harry
WALDIE, Margaret
WALKER, Jean
WALLACE, M.
WATERS, Isa
WATT, James A.*
WILSON, Netta
WRIGHT, Ina

1937

BARCLAY, H.
BOLES, Mary
CAIRNCROSS, George J.
FARTHING, H. Ross
FITZWALTER, Leslie
JOHNSTONE, W.
MURRAY, James W.
ROBERTSON, W.S.*
STEWART, E.
WRIGHT, Mr.*

1938

BAXTER, Stuart
CRAWFORD, Thomas P.
FOSTER, J.
HOBBS, David
HOGG, Adam R.
HOWARTH, George
JOHNSTON, G.W.
LANCASTER, Leslie
MILLER, W.
MURDOCH, A.
SHEPHERD, N.
STORMONT, Roland (Ronnie)
STORRIE, Mrs. T.
THOMPSON, S.
TURNBULL, William*

1939

AITKEN, Jessie (Cissie)
BERKELEY, R.
GOODYEAR, H.
LEITHEAD, R.
PRINGLE, Miss. N.
RUTHERFORD, Miss. E.
SALKELD, Miss. M.*
SMITH, Miss. M.J.M.
TOWNSEND, Miss. M.
TOWNSEND, Rena
TURNBULL, A.

1948

BALLANTYNE, W.
BARRON, Babs
BEATTIE, Maimie
COMBE, James
CURRIE, R.

ELLIOT, Leonard
FARRIES, Mary
FOX, Joe
GLADSTONE, T
HART, William
HELM, Peggy
HOBBS, Dorothy
HOGG, N.
HOWARTH, Betty
INGLIS, N.
KENNEDY, Elsie
KNIGHT, M.*
KYLE, I.
LAIDLAW, A.
LAING, Shiela
LYON, Audrey
MABLE, Margaret
MARTIN, Irene
MacDONALD, Ian
McHUGH, Sandra
MILLER, Charlotte
MORE, Albert*
MORGAN H. Grenville
ROBB, W. Cuthbert*
ROBERTSON, Margaret
ROBSON, Madge
RUSSELL, J.
STORRIE, T.
TELFER, Sadie
THOMSON, David
TURNBULL, Jean
TURNBULL, M.
TURNBULL, Mrs.*
TURNER, Maimie
WALDIE, Isabella
WALLACE, Miss.*
WHILLANS, Jean

1949

BURNETT, Betty
CHISHOLM, Margaret
CLARKE, Betty
CURRIE, Nessie
DOUGLAS, Kitty
DUNCAN, Lily
FABRICUS, Mr.*
FERGUSON, Margot
FORD, Jean
FOX, Mrs. Rose
GRAHAM, Betty
HOWARTH, Walter G.

HUNTER, Chrissie
INGLIS, Netta
LITTLE, Cathie
LONG, Laurie
ROBERTSON, Lydia
ROBSON, Nan
RUSSELL, Nan
SCOTT, Betty
SNOWDEN, Mr.*
WALSH, John

1950

ARMSTRONG, Eileen*
CUTHBERTSON, Betty
DUNNE, H.
FROUD, Muriel*
GWILSH, Mr.*
HAY, Cathie
KNOX, Margaret
LAW, June
McNAIRN, George
MILLAR, Grace
MURRAY, T.
NORMAN, P.*
RORRISON, Ian
SHIEL, H.
STORRIE, M.
WILKINSON, Maisie

1951

AITHEN, N.
ARMSTRONG, Robert
CAMPBELL, M. D.
KERSEL, Evelyn
RITCHIE, Paula F.
SCOTT, Margot
STAGE, J.

1952

ARMSTRONG, Tom
CAMPBELL, H.*
COLLIER, Margaret
COOPER, E.W.*
HOGG,Nessie
KINGHORN, John
McBURNIE, J.*
OVEREND, J.*
RALSTON, Jean
SCOTT Andrew C.

STORIE, Mary
STORIE, Sybil
WILLIAMS, J.*

1953

DOUGLAS, John
FAITHFUL, C.*
HIBBERT, Tom
LAURIE, W.*
MILES, Helen
NARDINI, Luigi*
NEILSON, Myra
PRINGLE, Vera
STODDART, B.*
TAIT, William I. (Bill)
WATSON, Jean
WHILLANS, Nan
WHITEHEAD, Eric A.©
WRIGHT, Ian
WRIGHT, L.*

1954

BLACKWOOD, Jan
CLUCAS, William*
COWPER, Gilbert
CROZIER, Maisie
DUTHIE, W.*
MOWAT, Olga
RICHARDSON, Maimie
SCOTT, Douglas
SMALL, B.*
STORIE, George
STORMONT, Patricia
TAYLOR, Tom

1955

BOYD, Shiona
COWPER, Lily
CROMBIE, Jill
GIBB, David
HANDYSIDE, Jardine
JOHNSTONE, Janette
JOHNSTONE, Margaret
McGLYNNE, Noreen
MILLIGAN, Charles
NICHOL, Jean
TODD, Margaret

1956

ARMSTRONG, Evelyn
BALDERSTONE, Mr.*
BENNETT, Carole
BROOMFIELD, Ella
BROWN, Marilyn
BURNS, Eric
CARLYLE, Douglas
CHANDLER, V.*
HARLEY, Kenneth
HODGINS, William
HOGG, Margaret
INGLIS, P.
JOHNSTONE, Maimie
KENNAWAY, Douglas
MILLAR, Jean
SLATER, Miss. B.*
SMITH, Charlotte
WALDIE, Maureen

1957

BLACK, Stewart
COMBE, Oliver
CUTHBERTSON, Janette
ELLIOT, Edith
FARQUHARSON, Moyra
FLEMING, Moira
GRAY, J.M.*
GREY, Catherine
HOGARTH, James
MANDERSON, Marion
RICHARDSON, Fraser
ROBSON, William (Bill)
SMITH, Maureen
STEWART, Morag
STILLIE, A.*
TURNBULL, George*
WHITE, Christine
WILSON, J.*

1958

ADAMSON, Vera
AITKEN, Arthur
ANDERSON, Peter
CRAWFORD, Ian
DICKSON, Eileen
ELLIS, Kenneth
KELSEY, Miss. J.M.*
REID, William

RENTON, William
ROBERTSON, Margaret
SCOTT, Eileen
SCOTT, Myra
TAYLOR, RITA
TURNBULL, Linda
WHITEHEAD, Dennis*

1959

ANDERSON, James
ARMSTRONG, Eileen
BALD, Ronald
COMBE, Carole
FARQUHARSON, Sandra
FLEMING, Shirley
GRAY, Douglas
HANNAH, Annette
LANCASTER, Evelyn
LOWES, Gwen
LYON, Christine
MITCHELL, Elsie
MURPHY, John
ROBSON, Ada
STEWART, Ella
SULLIVAN, Maureen
TAIT, Mary
TAYLOR, Ross
TIERNEY, B.
WATERS.B.
YELLOWLEES, I.

1960

AMOS, Sadie
ANDERSON, Joyce
BELL, Frances
BONSOR, J. Brian*
COWEN, Irene
DUCKWORTH, Fred
GALLOWAY, Margaret
HOGG, Patricia
JOHNSTON, Dorothy
KYLE, Jan
LAMOND, Margaret
LEESON, Lesley
LINDSAY, Cecilia
ORMISTON, Kay
PEDEN, Margaret
RAMAGE, Sandra
RENWICK, Doreen
ROBSON, June

RORRISON, Sheena
RUSSELL, Marjorie
RUSSELL, Myra
SCOTT, Netta
SLORANCE, Eileen
SMITH, Morag
SPALDING, Isa
SPINKS, Craig
SUTHERLAND, Dora

1961

ANDERSON, Nan
BIDMEAD, Anne
GRAHAM, Mrs. W.*
HARPER, Diana
HILL, Christine
HORNE, Peter
MATHER, Margaret
McGREGOR, J.*
SCOTT, D.*
SCOTT, Jacqueline
SOWERBUTTS, L.*
SULLIVAN, Margaret
WARWICK, Betty
WHYTE, Brenda
YOUNG, Mrs. R.*

1962

CAMPBELL, N.*
GORDON, William
JARDINE, Billy
JACKSON, Janette
OLIVER, Joseph
OLIVER, Maureen
PEACOCK, David
SCOTT, Ann
SCOTT, Robert
SHAW, Wallace
WATERS, Wilma
WYSE, William

1963

ALLAN, Andrew
DELGATTY, Eleanor
HUGHES, Anne
KINGHORN, Alistair
LAW, Helen
OLIVER, Shiela
REID, Ian

REILLY, Anne
ROSENKRANTZ, Diane
ROSENKRANTZ, Patricia
SCOTT, Patricia
SMITH, Eileen
SPALDING, C.*
WATSON, Kathleen

1964

ARMSTRONG, Robert
BARKER, Anne
BEATY, Anne
BEVAN, Mrs. V.*
CRAWFORD, Christine
CRAWFORD, Sheena
CURRAN, Miss. C.*
DOUGLAS, Morag
FLEMING, Anne
GRAHAM, Frances
GRAHAM, Norman
GREEN, Anne
HERD, Sandy
HOGG, Jennifer
KINGHORN, Shelagh
LINTON, Susan
LYLE, Patricia
McCARTNEY, Kenneth
McKAY, Derek
NICHOL, Margery
NICHOLS, L.*
RENWICK, Jim
ROMANES, A.*
SCOTT, Margaret
SMITH, Anne
WARWICK, Elizabeth
WINTROPE, Anne
YOUNG, David©
YOUNG, Dorothy
YOUNG, Pamela

1965

BAMFORTH, John
BRISBANE, Tommy
CANNON, Francis
HILL, Edward
LAIDLAW, George
PROUDFOOT, Janet
REID, Margaret

1966

DALGLEISH, A.*
DAUGHTRY, Irene
HUGGAN, Janette
McLEOD, Myra
MURRAY, Pat
OLIVER, Moira
REID, Margaret
ROBSON, Adam
SCOTT, Kathryn
SCOTT, Pat
SHEARMAN, Audrey

1967

COUPER, Claire
FORD, Alison
FUSARO, Carole
GASTON, Andy
MUIR, Jenny
RANDALLS, G.*
ROSS, James
WALKER, Ian*

1968

BOYLE, Miss.M.*
BRYANT, Mr.*
DALGLEISH, D.*
DOUGLAS, Dorothy P.
GRAY, Forbes
GRFFITHS, David©
LITTLE, Eileen
McLACHLAN, Fay
NIXON, Gerry
ROBSON, Joan
SLORANCE, Maureen
SMITH, Neil

1969

DALGLEISH, Letta
DEANS, Colin
DOUGLAS, John*
DRUMMOND, William A.*
FRASER, Graeme
McLACHLAN, Alison
MURDOCH, Anne
MURDOCH, Tom
MURPHY, Mr.*
ROWELL, Mary D.*
SMITH, Elizabeth

1970

BYERS, Billy
CAIRNS, I.*
CHARTERS, George*
COURT, C.*
DOUGLAS, Sandy
FINLAYSON, G.*
FRAME, Stewart
FULTON, Netta
HALLOWDEANE, Aaron
HARDY, D.*
MALONE, Mr.*
MILLIGAN, Anne
SHORT, Gordon
WYLIE, Ian
YOUNG, A.*

1971

ANDERSON, Gail
BOOKLESS, Louise
BROWN, Sandra
CORBETT, Colin
ELLIOT, Kim
HOGARTH, Deborah
HOWIESON, Elaine
MacKAY, David*
NICHOLS, Ruth
ROBSON, Sally
SCOTT, Dorothy
SCHMIDT, Elsie
SEELEY, Alison
THOMPSON, Rosalie
WALKER, Brian
WALKER, May
WINTROPE, Sybil

1972

BAPTIE, Bill*
BLACK, Jayne
CHAMBERS, Tom
CROWE, David T.
CROWE, Margaret
KELLY, Pauline*
MILLIGAN, George
POW, Alister
ROBSON, Joyce
WALLACE, Jim

1973

BALD, Angela
BALD, Jacqueline
BOWRING, Marion
DALGLEISH, Ellis
DALGLEISH, Norma
JAMIESON, Michael*
McCLYMONT, Elizabeth
ROBSON, Donald
SMITH, Sybil
TAIT, Margaret

1974

BROWN, George
ESSLEMONT, Patricia
HOGG, Edith
LUNN, Maureen
MARTIN, Edward
MORRISON, Graham
MURRAY, Shirley
SCOTT, Jacqueline
SCOTT, Susan
SEELEY, Ian W.*
SMAIL, Wilma
THOMPSON, Adrienne

1975

DICKSON, Ian
FORBES, Ian
GILCHRIST, Lynn
LAIDLAW, Sybil
McHUGH, John
MIDDLEMASS, Jack
SMITH, Marianne
WALLACE, David
WATSON, George

1976

BARKER, Julie
BROTHERSTON, Kenneth*
CHAMBERLAIN, Peter*
DUNSHEA, Janice
FLEMING, Richard*
FRASER, Andrew*
HOUGH, Wendy
HUGHES, Alan
JONES, Alison*
McLELLAND, Elspeth*

MILLIGAN, Donald*
MITCHELL, Christine
MURRAY, Carol
MURRAY, Gerald
NORTON, David*
SCOTT, Betty*

1977

ANDERSON, Ian
AITCHISON, Patricia
ARBON, Jim
GRAHAM, Muriel
JENKINS, Margaret*
JENKINS, Michael*
MARTIN, Fred
McCREDIE, Dorothy
McCREDIE, Kenneth
NARDINI, Marco
NARDINI, Nadia
RICHARDSON, R.*
ROBERTSON, Keith
SCOTT, Wendy
SLORANCE, Margaret
SMAIL, Miss. S.*
STORIE, Roger
WESTWATER, M.*
WHILLANS, Susan
WOODS, D.*

1978

AITKEN, Michael
BORTHWICK, Graham*
BORTHWICK, J.
COCKBURN, Anne
ELMITT, Michael*
HEWSON, Stephen*
KERR, R.*
McGLONE, Nessie
ROBERTSON, Pringle
STODDART, Harry

1979

BIRCH, Lacky*
BROATCH, Jane
BROWN, Louise
DEANE, Basil©
DICKSON, Morag
ELLIOT, Margaret
GRAY, Lesley

HATTON, Michael
HEWSON, Ken*
JACKSON, Katrina
KERR, Jane M.*
LAUDER, Alison
LITTLE, Karen
MACKIE, Donna
MACKIE, Karen
MATTHEWS, Jill
McCREDIE, Craig
MacDONALD, Donald
McGREGOR, Fiona
MURPHY, Noelle
MURRAY, Ruth
RENNIE, Jill
RIMMER, Jeffrey*
ROBERTSON, Morag
SEELEY, Melanie
SLORANCE, Graham
SLORANCE, Kerry
SLORANCE, Leah
STEWART, Deborah
STEWART, Diane
SUTHERLAND, Patricia
TURNBULL, Andrea

1980

NO SHOW

1981

BRANDON, Anita
CHISHOLM, Billy
COWAN, Christine*
FOX, Stephen©
KING, George
LARSON, Phil*
McRAE, Isaac*
McCREDIE, Keith
NELSON, Tony*
ROBERTSON, Fergus
SHAW, Ian*
SMITH, Ron
STEWART, Norma
WALSH, Robert

1982

BOOTH, Susan*
HORNE, Alison
LEWIS, Tony

McNAIRN, Fiona*
McNEIL, John*
ROBERTSON, Linda*
SCHEILHAN, Ulrika
SIMPSON, Fiona*
SMART, Jennifer
SMART, Sandra
WADDELL, Robert*

1983

BONTEAU, Christian
FRASER, Derek
FREYER, Bernd
GIBB, Drew*
KYLE, Linda
LOCKEAR, Christopher*
TOLLICK, Martin*
WATT, Rosemarie

1984

ANDERSON, Margaret
COCKBURN, L.*
DUNNE, Ralph
ESSLEMONT, Peter
ESSLEMONT, William
FARMER, Lesley
FORBES, Rowena*
GOLDIE, Elliot
HORNE, Margaret
LESLIE, Elizabeth
MAULE, Harriet
MUNRO, Andrea
MURPHY, Adrienne
REID, Andrew (Andy)
REPNER, Josef
STORIE, Alan
STORMONT, Lesley
THOMSON, Fiona
WALKER, Alice
WILSON, Alastair
WRIGHT, William

1985

CROWE, Elizabeth
FARRIES, Rob
FERGUSON, Edward A.©
GANNON, Derek
HOGARTH, Campbell
LESLIE, Brian

LESLIE, Victoria
McGINN, Stuart
STORMONT, David

1986

COWAN, Alex
DEVINE, Des
GILLESPIE, Anne
MARSHALL, David*
McKENZIE, Ian
MILNE, Neil
NEILL, David*
ROBERTSON, Peter
SNEDDON, Les
STORIE, Alfie
STORIE, Julie
TREACY, Steve
TURNBULL, Shelagh
WRIGHT, Cameron

1987

GIBSON, Stuart
JEARY, Lynne*
LAWSON, Karen
MATTHEW, Louise*
MAYNES,Charles*
SANGER, Linsay
STORIE, Vanessa
WANDS, Alex*
WATSON, David*

1988

BLACKLOCK, Margaret
CAIN, Helen*
CAMPBELL, Murray*
CHAMBERLAIN, Bridget*
COCKBURN, Kathryn
DEVLIN, Hazel
GREGORY, Fiona*
GREGORY, Kate*
HARDIE, Ian J.*
JENKINS, Anne*
MAYNES, Valerie A.*
McCREDIE, Lyndsay
ODDY, Zilla
SCOTT, Iain
SLORANCE, Adele
SLORANCE, Tanya
THOMPSON, Alistair

THOMSON, Helen*
YOUNG, Rona

1989

ACHENBACH, Chris*
BROWN, Tracy*
COMELY, Neil
HARVEY, Bill
HAY, Sophie*
HUME, Robert*
KEMP, Colin*
KERR, Rob*
MEECHAN, Dorothy
ROMFREY, David

1990

BUNYAN, Carol
KYLE, Lesley
LAIDLAW, Eric*
LYONS, Asha
MAAS, Anne*
RODGERSON, Ian
SCOTT, Robert*
TOLSON, Arthur*
TURNBULL, Audrey

1991

BARKER, Frank
COULSON, Graham
FISHER, Susan
HEADSPEATH, Jane
KENNEDY, Stuart
McSHERRY, Marie
PARKER, Olive
PIGGOT, Kenny
RENWICK, Scott
ROBSON, Frances
ROSANNO, Nick
TYRRELL, Robbie
WHITE, Margaret

1992

CALDER, Derek
REID, John
STRICKLAND, Christopher*
TURNBULL, Mark

136

1993

BLACKLOCK, Laura
BURKE, Ian
CLAY, Katy
LILLEY, Steve*
McCRAW, Bill
PENDER, Kim
SHARKEY, Linda
TAIT, Lorna

1994

MELROSE, Gordon*

1995

BAILEY, Niall*
BORTHWICK, Jan
CHEEK, Jim*
COE, Sam*
CROSBY, Malcolm
DALGLEISH, Susan
DOUGLAS, Anne
GOLDIE, Rob
JOHNSTONE, Graeme
KELLAS, David*
McINTYRE, Roddy*
McKENDRICK, ANNE*
MUIR, Kit*
MYTHEN, Barbara*
NEWMAN, Claire
RAMANES, Brian
ROBERTSON, Elaine*
RODKISS, Tracy

1996

CROSBY, Susan
DUNCAN, Ian
GESIERICH, Ulrike*
HOWDEN, Richard*
HUME, Kathryn*
KINSELLA, Laureen
MILLER, Robin*
MOONEY, James*
PATTERSON, Gillian
ROUX, Fabien*
SQUANCE, Steven
TODD, Joy*

1997

COUND, Mike
FIRTH, James*
MORE, Jonathan*

1998

BACON, Brian
BROWN, Steve
CAIN, Louise*
ELLIS, Jonathan
FOX, Colin©
FRASER, Graham*
GORMAN, Ruth*
HOWDEN, Chris*
PATERSON, Catriona

1999(A)

BLAIKIE, Angela*
BLAIKIE, Colin*
BLAKE, Angela*
BLAKE, Suzanne*
BOLES, Helen
DEANE, Jennifer*
DOUGLAS, Nicola*
FOWLER, John
HUNTER, Sonia*
INGLIS, Jim
INGLIS, Nancy*
JENKINSON, Glen
KERR, Victoria*
LETHAM, James©
McDONALD, Liam*
MURRAY, Andrew*
MURRAY, Greg*
MURRAY, Julie
NORMAN, Ruth*
PATERSON, Susan
RENWICK, David
RENWICK, Lindsey
SCOTT, Rhona
TIERNEY, Paul*

1999(B)

ANDERSON, Bill
ANDERSON, William
BRADSHAW, Lynne*
FLAVIN, Marie-Louise*
FOGGO, Tom*

HINTON, Lynne
HUTCHINS, Sam*
NEILSON, Craig
PATERSON, Heather
ROSE, Les*
WARD, Danny*

2000

ANDERSON, Laura
COUND, Sasha
LOVE, Catriona*
McCREDIE, Lyndsay
MILLER, Scott*
MURRAY, Michael
RALLY, Charles*
STORMONT, Leanne
WALKER, Pamela*

2001

CLARK, Annabelle
CROSBY, Angela
DUNN, Laawrence*
ELLIOT-WALKER, Emma
GILLIES, Victoria
GRAHAM, Rhianna
HALL, Adam
HAMILTON, Graham*
INGLIS, Rachel
LIGHTFOOT,Harry jnr.
MacFARLANE, Lynsey
McGILL, Scott*
MacKAY, Louise
McKEAN, Andrew
McLEOD, Louise
MILLER, Rachel
MITCHELL, Ross
MITCHELL,Stuart
MOORE, Tara
NIBLO, Lois
NICHOL, Samantha
PATERSON, Natalie
RAFFERTY, Emily
RAYNER, Mandy,
REID, Lyn
SOLLEY, Owen
TORRIE, Lana

2002

CASSON, Pamela
CORMIE, Cath*

DORWARD, Ruth
GORDON, Graham
INGLIS, Derek
NASKAR, Manab*
NORMAN, Paul*
RAMAGE, Lisa*

2003

ANDERSON, Christine*
BELL, Rowan*
HARRIS, Alison*
LONGMUIR, Ruth*
MacFADYEN, Iain*
MALLIN, Janie
SCOBIE, Colin*

2004

BAIN, Morag
BROTHERSTON, Ian
CASSON, Megan
ELLIOT-WALKER, Isla
HALLIDAY, Ellen
HARRIS, Alison*
JAVIER, Justin
MacFARLANE, Robbie
MUIR, Nancy*
PURVIS, Hazel
SZONEBERG, Louise
WATSON, Ron
WHINHAM, Karen

2005

ANDERSON, Sandra
CAMPBELL, Niall
CASWELL, Liam
HOGART, James*
HUNTER, Andrew
KIME, Tony*
KIRK, Jonathan
LOCKIE, Paul
SCOTT, Jamie

2006

AITKIN, Ross
TOTTMAN, Lee

2007

WALKER, Howard
WILKINSON, Ashley

2008

CASSON, Lyn
LAW, Jo
LAW, Steven
NOBLE, Anne*
PATERSON, Robert
RANDALL, Tony
SHERWOOD, Adam

2009

CAIRNS, Emma
HART, Jason
HUGGAN, Sean
HYSLOP, Fergus
INGLIS, Claire
INGLIS, Louise
KYLE, Craig
LAW, Emma
MILLAN, Richard
MILLIGAN, Ross*
OLIVER, Clare
PATERSON, David
WILKINSON, Caroline

2010

REDMAN, Ben*
ROONEY, Billy

Hawick Amateur Operatic Society gratefully acknowledges financial assistance with this publication from the National Lottery Fund, Hawick Archaeological Society, Hawick Callants' Club, Hawick Gilded Chamber and The Rotary Club of Hawick.